BRIDGING GRADES

4 to 5

CARSON-DELLOSA®
PUBLISHING GROUP

Greensboro, NC 27425 USA

Caution: Exercise activities may require adult supervision. Before beginning any exercise activity, consult a physician. Written parental permission is suggested for those using this book in group situations. Children should always warm up prior to beginning any exercise activity and should stop immediately if they feel any discomfort during exercise.

Caution: Before beginning any food activity, ask parents' permission and inquire about the child's food allergies and religious or other food restrictions.

Caution: Nature activities may require adult supervision. Before beginning any nature activity, ask parents' permission and inquire about the child's plant and animal allergies. Remind the child not to touch plants or animals during the activity without adult supervision.

Caution: Before completing any balloon activity, ask parents' permission and inquire about possible latex allergies. Also, remember that uninflated or popped balloons may present a choking hazard.

The authors and publisher are not responsible or liable for any injury that may result from performing the exercises or activities in this book.

Summer Bridge®
An imprint of Carson-Dellosa Publishing LLC
PO Box 35665
Greensboro, NC 27425 USA
carsondellosa.com

Printed in the USA • All rights reserved.

ISBN 978-1-4838-1584-8

11-105191151

Table of Contents

About Summer Learning

Did you know that many children experience learning loss when they do not engage in educational activities during the summer? This means that some of what they have spent time learning over the preceding school year is forgotten during the summer months. However, summer learning loss is something that you can help prevent. Below are a few suggestions for fun and engaging activities that can help children maintain and grow their academic skills during the summer.

- Read with your child every day. Visit your local library together and select books on subjects that interest your child.

- Ask your child's teacher to recommend books for summer reading.

- Explore parks, nature preserves, museums, and cultural centers.

- Look for teachable moments every day. Measuring ingredients for recipes and reviewing maps before a car trip are fun and useful ways to learn or reinforce skills.

- Each day, set goals for your child to accomplish. For example, complete five math problems or read one section or chapter in a book.

- Encourage your child to complete the activities in this book regularly to help bridge the summer learning gap.

About Summer Bridge Activities®

The learning activities in this book are designed to review fourth grade skills, preview the skills your child will learn in fifth grade, and help prevent summer learning loss. Your involvement in your child's education is crucial to his or her success. Together with *Summer Bridge Activities*, you can fill the summer months with learning experiences that will deepen and enrich your child's knowledge and prepare him or her for the upcoming school year. Inside this book, you will find the following helpful resources:

Three sections that correspond to the three months of a traditional summer vacation. Each section begins with a goal-setting activity, a word list, and information about the fitness and character development activities located throughout the section.

Learning activity pages. For maximum results, your child should complete two activity pages each day. These engaging, age-appropriate activities cover a range of subjects including reading comprehension, writing, grammar skills, fractions, decimals, geometry, and more. Each page is numbered by day, and each day includes a space to place a motivational sticker when the activities are complete.

Bonus outdoor learning experiences, science experiments, and social studies exercises. These fun and creative activities are found at the end of each section. Complete the pages with your child throughout each month as time allows.

Flash cards. Help your child cut out these handy cards and use them for practice anytime and anywhere. For children who are entering fifth grade, use the cards to:

- Match homophones (words such as *sea* and *see* that sound alike but have different meanings and spellings).
- Match synonyms (words with similar meanings) and antonyms (words with opposite meanings).
- Learn words with Latin and Greek roots.
- Understand mathematical expressions in words and numbers.
- Multiply and divide decimal numbers.
- Use place value to understand decimal numbers in expanded form. For example, $152.25 = (1 \times 100) + (5 \times 10) + (2 \times 1) + (2 \times \frac{1}{10}) + (5 \times \frac{1}{100})$.
- Multiply fractions.
- Form equivalent fractions.
- Calculate volume.

Certificate of completion. At the end of the summer, fill out the certificate and present it to your child to celebrate learning success!

Stickers. Demonstrate how to place a sticker in the space provided to show that each day's learning activities are complete. Praise your child's effort!

Online companion. Visit *summerlearningactivities.com/sba* with your child to find even more fun and creative ways to prevent summer learning loss.

Skills Matrix

Day	Addition	Data Analysis	Division	Fitness & Character Education	Fractions	Geometry	Grammar	Language Arts	Measurement	Mixed Math Practice	Multiplication	Puzzles	Reading Comprehension	Science	Social Studies	Subtraction	Time & Money	Vocabulary	Word Problems	Writing
1				★				★		★										
2								★			★		★							
3							★	★		★							★			
4						★		★					★							
5							★	★		★										
6							★	★		★										
7					★								★							★
8							★	★	★											
9							★						★					★		
10								★			★				★			★		
11			★				★	★		★										
12	★					★			★			★								
13			★			★							★							
14					★	★		★										★		
15					★	★										★				★
16					★			★		★										
17								★					★					★		
18								★	★											★
19								★					★					★	★	
20				★	★										★					
BONUS PAGES!				★									★	★	★					★
1				★				★												★
2			★					★	★		★									
3						★		★										★		
4								★					★							★
5		★						★		★										
6								★		★			★							
7								★		★										
8			★						★							★		★		
9			★					★												★
10						★								★	★					
11					★			★		★				★						

Skills Matrix

Day	Addition	Data Analysis	Division	Fitness & Character Education	Fractions	Geometry	Grammar	Language Arts	Measurement	Mixed Math Practice	Multiplication	Puzzles	Reading Comprehension	Science	Social Studies	Subtraction	Time & Money	Vocabulary	Word Problems	Writing
12								★			★		★							
13			★	★			★													
14		★		★				★												★
15								★		★			★							
16							★	★						★						
17					★								★					★		
18								★		★										★
19					★		★			★										★
20							★	★											★	★
		★						BONUS PAGES!						★	★					★
1				★			★						★							
2					★			★				★								
3							★						★							★
4					★				★					★				★		
5		★											★							
6										★			★							★
7								★											★	★
8						★		★					★							
9		★						★		★								★		
10								★	★					★						
11								★	★				★							
12								★		★										★
13									★				★					★		
14							★						★							★
15						★		★					★							
16						★		★									★			
17				★					★										★	★
18								★		★			★							
19		★		★				★												
20												★	★							
			★					BONUS PAGES!						★	★					★

Encouraging Summer Reading

Literacy is the single most important skill that your child needs to be successful in school. The following list includes ideas for ways that you can help your child discover the great adventures of reading!

- Establish a time for reading each day. Ask your child about what he or she is reading. Try to relate the material to a summer event or to another book.

- Let your child see you reading for enjoyment. Talk about the great things that you discover when you read.

- Create a summer reading list. Choose books from the reading list (pages ix–x) or head to the library and explore. Ask your child to read a page from a book aloud. If he or she does not know more than five words on the page, the book may be too difficult.

- Read newspaper and magazine articles, recipes, menus, and maps on a daily basis to show your child the importance of reading for information.

- Choose a nonfiction book from the reading list that is a firsthand account of an event or of a person's life, such as Peter Sís's autobiography *The Wall*. Then, search at the library or online to find a secondhand account of the same events. How are the two accounts similar? How are they different?

- Choose a nonfiction book to read or reread with your child. Then, have him or her pretend to be a TV reporter, sharing the "news" of the book you read. Encourage your child to relate details and events from the story in the report.

- Make up stories. This is especially fun to do in the car, on camping trips, or while waiting at the airport. Encourage your child to tell a story with a beginning, a middle, and an end. Or, have your child start a story and let other family members build on it.

- Encourage your child to join a summer reading club at the library or a local bookstore. Your child may enjoy talking to other children about the books that he or she has read.

- Encourage your child to read several books from a favorite genre, such as mystery or science fiction. Discuss how different books treat similar themes.

- Ask your child to think about a favorite character from a book or series of books. How might that character respond to different situations?

Summer Reading List

The summer reading list includes fiction and nonfiction titles. Experts recommend that fourth- and fifth-grade children read for at least 25 to 30 minutes each day. Then, ask questions about the story to reinforce comprehension.

Decide on an amount of daily reading time for each month. You may want to write the time on the Monthly Goals page at the beginning of each section in this book.

Fiction

Barshaw, Ruth McNally
Ellie McDoodle: Have Pen, Will Travel

Baum, L. Frank (adapted by Michael Cavallaro)
L. Frank Baum's The Wizard of Oz: The Graphic Novel

Blume, Judy
Superfudge

Cherry, Lynne and Mark J. Plotkin
The Shaman's Apprentice: A Tale of the Amazon Rain Forest

Cleary, Beverly
Henry and the Clubhouse
Henry Huggins
Ramona's World
Ribsy

Collins, Suzanne
Underland Chronicles (series)

Dahl, Roald
The BFG
Charlie and the Chocolate Factory

DeJong, Meindert
The House of Sixty Fathers

DiCamillo, Kate
Because of Winn-Dixie
Flora & Ulysses

du Bois, William Pène
The Twenty-One Balloons

Fitzgerald, Laura Marx
Under the Egg

Fox, Paula
Maurice's Room

Goble, Paul
The Girl Who Loved Wild Horses

Grabenstein, Chris
Escape from Mr. Lemoncello's Library

Heard, Georgia (ed.)
Falling Down the Page: A Book of List Poems

Juster, Norton
The Phantom Tollbooth

Levine, Ellen
Henry's Freedom Box: A True Story from the Underground Railroad

Lewis, C. S.
The Lion, the Witch and the Wardrobe

Martin, Ann M.
A Dog's Life: The Autobiography of a Stray

Morse, Scott
Magic Pickle

O'Brien, Robert C.
Mrs. Frisby and the Rats of NIMH

Summary Reading List (continued)

Fiction (continued)

O'Dell, Scott
Island of the Blue Dolphins

O'Malley, Kevin
Once Upon a Cool Motorcycle Dude

Paulsen, Gary
Lawn Boy

Rowling, J. K.
Harry Potter and the Sorcerer's Stone

Rylant, Cynthia
Missing May

Sachar, Louis
Sideways Stories from Wayside School

Silverstein, Shel
Where the Sidewalk Ends

Tooke, Wes
King of the Mound: My Summer with Satchel Paige

Van Allsburg, Chris
Jumanji

Waters, Kate
Tapenum's Day: A Wampanoag Indian Boy in Pilgrim Times

White, E. B.
Charlotte's Web
Stuart Little
The Trumpet of the Swan

Wilder, Laura Ingalls
Little House on the Prairie

Nonfiction

Cate, Annette LeBlanc
Look Up!: Bird-Watching in Your Own Backyard

Cherry, Lynne and Gary Braasch
How We Know What We Know About Our Changing Climate: Scientists and Kids Explore Global Warming

Colbert, David
10 Days: Martin Luther King Jr.

Dyer, Alan
Mission to the Moon

Hill, Laban Carrick
When the Beat Was Born: DJ Kool Herc and the Creation of Hip Hop

MacLeod, Elizabeth and Frieda Wishinsky
A History of Just About Everything: 180 Events, People and Inventions That Changed the World

Nicklin, Flip and Linda
Face to Face with Dolphins

Pratt-Serafini, Kristin Joy and Rachel Crandell
The Forever Forest: Kids Save a Tropical Treasure

Robbins, Ken
Thunder on the Plains: The Story of the American Buffalo

Roberts, Cokie
Founding Mothers

Sís, Peter
The Wall: Growing Up Behind the Iron Curtain

Monthly Goals

A goal is something that you want to accomplish. Sometimes, reaching a goal can be hard work!

Think of three goals to set for yourself this month. For example, you may want to learn three new vocabulary words each week. Write your goals on the lines and review them with an adult.

Place a sticker next to each goal that you complete. Feel proud that you have met your goals!

1. _____ PLACE STICKER HERE

2. _____ PLACE STICKER HERE

3. _____ PLACE STICKER HERE

Word List

The following words are used in this section. They are good words for you to know. Read each word aloud. Use a dictionary to look up each word that you do not know. Then, write two sentences. Use a word from the word list in each sentence.

energy	interpret
factor	knowledge
government	leaders
healthy	passage

1. _____

_____

2. _____

_____

Introduction to Flexibility

This section includes fitness and character development activities that focus on flexibility. These activities are designed to get you moving and thinking about building your physical fitness and your character.

Physical Flexibility

For many people, being flexible means easily doing everyday tasks, such as bending to tie a shoe. Tasks like this can be hard for people who do not stretch often.

Stretching will make your muscles more flexible. It can also improve your balance and coordination.

You probably stretch every day without realizing it. Do you ever reach for a dropped pencil or a box of cereal on the top shelf? If you do, then you are stretching. Try to improve your flexibility this summer. Set a stretching goal. For example, you might stretch every day until you can touch your toes.

Flexibility of Character

It is good to have a flexible body. It is also good to be mentally flexible. This means being open to change.

It can be upsetting when things do not go your way. Can you think of a time when an unexpected event ruined your plans? For example, a family trip to the zoo was canceled because the car had a flat tire. Unexpected events happen sometimes. How you react to those events often affects the outcome. Arm yourself with the tools to be flexible. Have realistic expectations. Find ways to make the situation better. Look for good things that may have come from the event.

You can be mentally flexible by showing respect to other people. Sharing and taking turns are also ways to be mentally flexible. This character trait gets easier with practice. Over the summer, practice and use your mental flexibility often.

Solve each problem.

1. 13 – 5 = _____
2. 15 – 9 = _____
3. 4 × 3 = _____

4. 9 + 2 = _____
5. 10 ÷ 2 = _____
6. 6 + 4 = _____

7. 6 × 5 = _____
8. 30 ÷ 6 = _____
9. 13 + 5 = _____

10. 17 – 9 = _____
11. 3 × 6 = _____
12. 27 ÷ 3 = _____

Find each missing number.

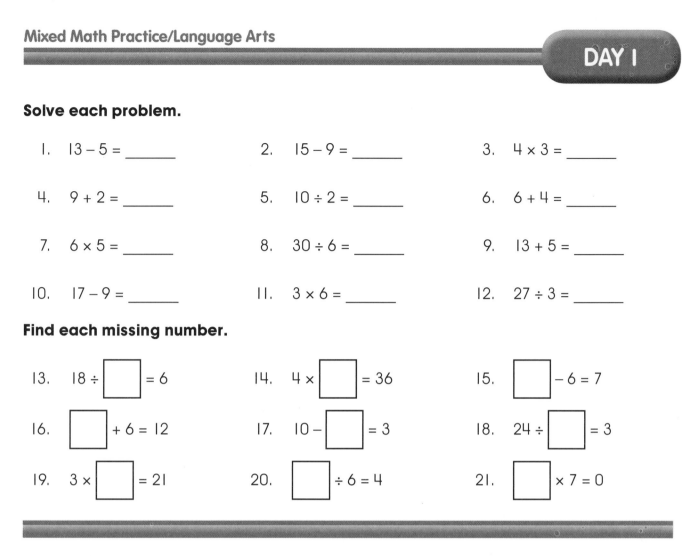

13. 18 ÷ ☐ = 6
14. 4 × ☐ = 36
15. ☐ – 6 = 7

16. ☐ + 6 = 12
17. 10 – ☐ = 3
18. 24 ÷ ☐ = 3

19. 3 × ☐ = 21
20. ☐ ÷ 6 = 4
21. ☐ × 7 = 0

A sentence is a group of words that expresses a complete thought. Write *yes* before each group of words if it is a sentence. Write *no* if the group is not a sentence.

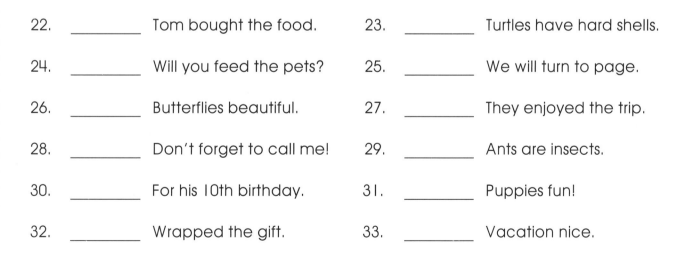

22. _____ Tom bought the food.
23. _____ Turtles have hard shells.

24. _____ Will you feed the pets?
25. _____ We will turn to page.

26. _____ Butterflies beautiful.
27. _____ They enjoyed the trip.

28. _____ Don't forget to call me!
29. _____ Ants are insects.

30. _____ For his 10th birthday.
31. _____ Puppies fun!

32. _____ Wrapped the gift.
33. _____ Vacation nice.

DAY 1

A thesaurus is a reference book that contains synonyms and antonyms. In each row, circle the word that does not belong.

34. family   tribe   clan   enemy

35. time   Earth   globe   sphere

36. notice   overlook   observe   see

37. sky   sun   orb   planet

Stretch Your Limits

If you are going to a pool, a beach, or a lake to cool off this summer, try doing a post-swimming stretch called the *cobra stretch*. Lie on your stomach with your legs stretched behind you. The soles of your feet should be facing up. Place your hands on the ground under your shoulders. Keep your elbows close to your body. As you take a deep breath, push your hands into the ground and lift your chest as high as is comfortable. Relax and look up slightly, stretching your lower back and breathing easily. Hold the stretch for 20 seconds.

FACTOID: Ladybugs chew their food from side to side, not up and down.

* See page ii.

4

PLACE STICKER HERE

DAY 2

Add quotation marks and commas where they are needed.

1. I love going to the natural history museum! exclaimed Ananya.

2. I usually go see the animals first replied Noah and then I go to the planetarium.

3. Have you seen the dinosaur fossils? asked Eliza.

4. She added The dioramas of prehistoric life are really cool.

5. That's my favorite part said Antonio.

6. Did you know that I'm one-quarter Native American? asked Dylan.

7. That's why I like the display of Native American artifacts he said.

8. Let's start out with the western life display suggested Mira and then head over to the planetarium.

Write all factor pairs for each number.

9. **16**

_____ × _____

_____ × _____

_____ × _____

10. **15**

_____ × _____

_____ × _____

11. **36**

_____ × _____

_____ × _____

_____ × _____

_____ × _____

_____ × _____

12. **42**

_____ × _____

_____ × _____

_____ × _____

_____ × _____

13. **24**

_____ × _____

_____ × _____

_____ × _____

_____ × _____

14. **99**

_____ × _____

_____ × _____

_____ × _____

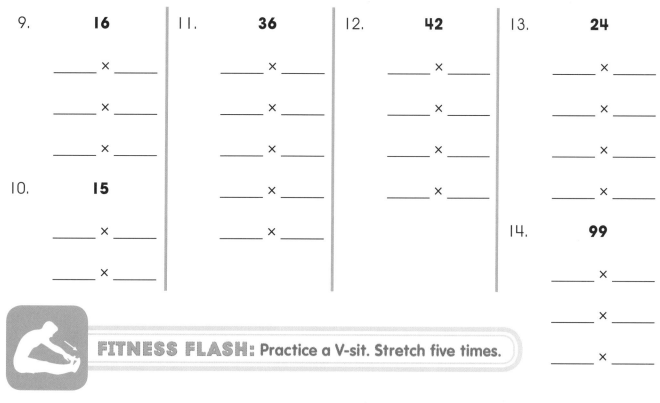

FITNESS FLASH: Practice a V-sit. Stretch five times.

* See page ii.

DAY 2

Read the passage. Then, answer the questions.

Giant Sequoias

The first giant sequoia trees probably started growing in North America about 180 million years ago. Giant sequoia trees can live more than 3,000 years. For the first 250 years, giant sequoias look like small pine trees. They reach their full height when they are about 500 years old. The giant sequoia can grow as tall as a 25-story building—that's about 250 feet (76 m) tall! Some trees have grown up to 30 feet (9 m) wide, or as wide as a three-lane highway. The largest giant sequoia living today is named General Sherman. General Sherman is over 274 feet (83 m) tall.

There are not many sequoias alive today. Millions of years ago, sequoias grew across North America. Then, the weather turned colder. These trees needed the warm weather to live. Now, when people visit the remaining sequoia forests, they drive and walk over the ground. This makes the ground hard. The sequoias' roots have a difficult time absorbing water in the hard ground. This is killing some of the trees. However, some people take home seeds when they visit the sequoia forests. They plant the seeds all over the world. Someday, these seeds may develop into new forests.

15. How long does it take a giant sequoia tree to reach its full height? _____

16. How tall is the largest giant sequoia tree living today? _____

17. Why are fewer giant sequoias alive today than in the past? _____

_____

_____

18. What are two things that giant sequoias need in order to survive? _____

_____

19. What details does the author provide to support the topic sentence of the second paragraph?

_____

PLACE STICKER HERE

When estimating numbers, round each number to the nearest place value before adding or subtracting. Estimate the sums and differences.

EXAMPLE:

$81 + 75 \approx$	1. $93 - 12 \approx$	2. $98 - 12 \approx$
80 + **80** = **160**	_____ − _____ = _____	_____ − _____ = _____
3. $93 - 39 \approx$	4. $891 - 551 \approx$	5. $57 - 39 \approx$
_____ − _____ = _____	_____ − _____ = _____	_____ − _____ = _____
6. $24 + 35 \approx$	7. $209 + 179 \approx$	8. $64 + 39 \approx$
_____ + _____ = _____	_____ + _____ = _____	_____ + _____ = _____

Circle the relative pronoun in each sentence. Then, write two sentences of your own that use relative pronouns.

9.   The boys who live next door to me have a playful brown dog.

10.   My grandpa, who lives in Michigan, likes to fix up old cars.

11.   The sweater that I borrowed from Elena has a hole in it.

12.   The Greek Festival, which takes place in August, is held at the convention center.

13.   Daniel's e-mail, which I received yesterday, includes the schedule for his trip.

14.   The dress that you bought today is similar to mine.

15.   The piano students, whose teacher is Mr. Randall, will be performing at 8:00.

16.   The bees that we ordered last spring seem to be doing very well.

17.   _____

18.   _____

DAY 3

There are 24 hours in a day. The times from midnight through 11:59 in the morning are written A.M., and the times from noon through 11:59 at night are written P.M. Write the correct times.

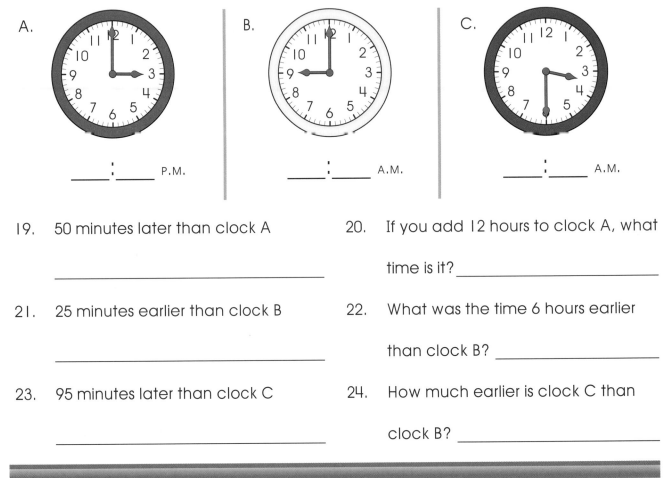

A.

_____:_____ P.M.

B.

_____:_____ A.M.

C.

_____:_____ A.M.

19. 50 minutes later than clock A

_____

20. If you add 12 hours to clock A, what

time is it? _____

21. 25 minutes earlier than clock B

_____

22. What was the time 6 hours earlier

than clock B? _____

23. 95 minutes later than clock C

_____

24. How much earlier is clock C than

clock B? _____

Add the missing commas to the compound sentences.

25. Natalia missed the bus so her stepdad drove her to school.

26. The male cardinal landed on the feeder and its mate joined it a moment later.

27. Ian is going ice-skating on Saturday and Abby is going to a birthday party.

28. We planned to cook out tonight but it looks like it's going to storm.

29. Xander has a lot of homework so we're not going to the movies.

30. The deer crossed the road and her two fawns followed.

8

PLACE STICKER HERE

Use what you know about polygons to make a pattern. Start with one polygon, and flip, turn, or slide it to make a pattern.

EXAMPLE:

Rewrite this address correctly.

1461 condor st

mr greg jones

lake tona oh

98562

FITNESS FLASH: Do arm circles for 30 seconds.

* See page ii.

DAY 4

Read the passage. Then, answer the questions.

Astronomers

Astronomy is the study of planets, stars, and the universe. The first astronomers were ancient people who observed star patterns called *constellations*. They gave them names, such as the Great Bear. Today, astronomers seek to learn about the universe. They use powerful telescopes to see stars and to measure their distance from Earth and the speed at which they are moving. Astronomers interpret data collected by satellites and spacecrafts. By using readings from different instruments, astronomers can predict when objects such as comets and meteors will appear in the night sky. Sometimes, astronomers discover new things in outer space. Halley's Comet, which can be seen every 76 years, was named after Edmond Halley, the astronomer who predicted that the comet would return in 1758. The names of modern astronomical discoveries must be approved by the International Astronomical Union, a professional organization for astronomers.

1. What is the main idea of this passage?

    a. Astronomers look at constellations of stars.

    b. Astronomers study objects in outer space.

    c. Some astronomers discover new comets.

2. What is astronomy?_____

3. Why do astronomers use telescopes?_____

4. What do astronomers try to predict using different instruments? _____

    _____

5. This is a secondhand account about what astronomers do. How would a firsthand account written by an astronomer be different? Which would you rather read? Why?

    _____

    _____

PLACE STICKER HERE

Write a sentence that includes a verb in the progressive tense (a form of *be* + verb + *ing*) to answer each question.

EXAMPLE: What were you doing at this time yesterday?
I **was washing** my dad's car.

1.   What will you be doing at 8:00 tomorrow morning?

_____

2.   What are you reading today?

_____

3.   What will you eat for lunch tomorrow?

_____

4.   What were you watching on TV yesterday?

_____

Answer each question.

5.   In a newspaper or magazine, find and circle two numbers. Write each number in word form, standard form, and expanded form.

_____

_____

6.   Write a sentence about the important role that numbers play in your daily life. Why is it important to be able to recognize the same number written in different forms?

_____

_____

DAY 5

Solve each problem.

| 7. | 428 − 119 | 8. | 4,918 + 3,928 | 9. | 248 + 48 | 10. | 569 − 247 |

| 11. | 2,709 + 1,282 | 12. | 304 − 172 | 13. | 143 + 219 | 14. | 681 + 145 |

The word *their* shows ownership, and the word *there* shows a place. Complete each sentence with *their* or *there*.

15. I left my coat _____ yesterday.

16. Ian and Mackenzie were training _____ horses to jump.

17. We are going to _____ farm tomorrow.

18. Please put the box over_____ .

19. Will you please sit here, not _____ ?

Write two sentences about your school. Use *their* in one sentence and *there* in the other.

20. _____

21. _____

CHARACTER CHECK: Think of a time when you did something nice for a friend or family member. How did that make you feel?

PLACE STICKER HERE

A suffix is added to the end of a base word. When some suffixes are added, it is necessary to double the base word's final consonant or change *y* to *i*. Add the suffix *-est* to the end of each base word and write the new word.

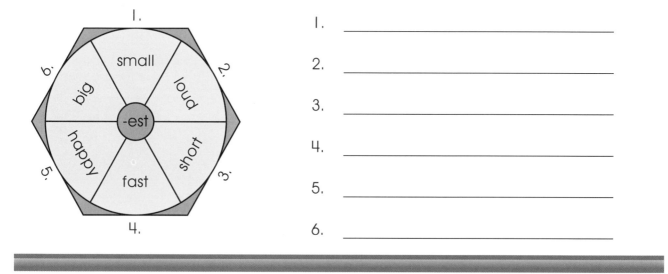

1. _____

2. _____

3. _____

4. _____

5. _____

6. _____

Homophones are words that sound the same but are spelled differently. Write five sentences. Use a pair of homophones from the word bank in each sentence. Underline the homophones.

no, know	sun, son	tail, tale	new, knew
way, weigh	sent, cent	sale, sail	their, there
ate, eight	see, sea	pair, pear	blew, blue

EXAMPLE:

Would you chop some wood?

7. _____

8. _____

9. _____

10. _____

11. _____

DAY 6

Write a description for each object using the adjectives in parentheses. Read each description to yourself to make sure the adjectives are in the correct order.

EXAMPLE: sweater (brown wool cozy)   **cozy brown wool sweater**

12. balls (beach four striped)   _____

13. basket (antique seagrass)   _____

14. mug (yellow ceramic)   _____

15. rock (rough gray)   _____

16. trucks (six red plastic small)   _____

17. tomato (plump juicy)   _____

18. dog (stray white)   _____

Complete each number pattern. Identify the rule used to create the pattern.

19. 3, 6, 5, 8, 7, 10, 9, _____, _____

Rule: _____

20. 1, 2, 4, 7, 11, 16, 22, _____, _____

Rule: _____

21. 2, 4, 6, 10, 16, 26, _____, _____

Rule: _____

FITNESS FLASH: Touch your toes 10 times.

* See page ii.

14

PLACE
STICKER
HERE

Add to find each sum. Write answers in simplest form.

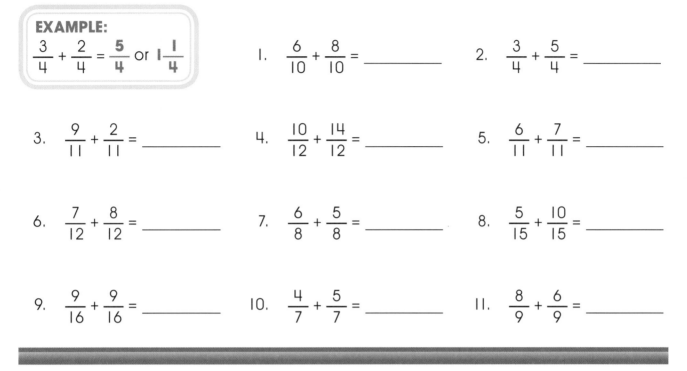

EXAMPLE:

$$\frac{3}{4} + \frac{2}{4} = \frac{5}{4} \text{ or } 1\frac{1}{4}$$

1. $\frac{6}{10} + \frac{8}{10} = $ _____

2. $\frac{3}{4} + \frac{5}{4} = $ _____

3. $\frac{9}{11} + \frac{2}{11} = $ _____

4. $\frac{10}{12} + \frac{14}{12} = $ _____

5. $\frac{6}{11} + \frac{7}{11} = $ _____

6. $\frac{7}{12} + \frac{8}{12} = $ _____

7. $\frac{6}{8} + \frac{5}{8} = $ _____

8. $\frac{5}{15} + \frac{10}{15} = $ _____

9. $\frac{9}{16} + \frac{9}{16} = $ _____

10. $\frac{4}{7} + \frac{5}{7} = $ _____

11. $\frac{8}{9} + \frac{6}{9} = $ _____

Read the five steps of the writing process to write a story.

A. Plan

B. First draft

C. Revise

D. Proofread

E. Final draft

Use the steps to finish the story on a separate sheet of paper.

You go for a walk one day and find a large, golden egg with green spots. Suddenly, it begins to shake and crack.

_____

_____

_____

FACTOID: There are more than 950 species of bats in the world.

DAY 7

Read the passage. Then, answer the questions.

Reptiles and Amphibians

You may think that lizards and frogs are in the same family, but they are not. Lizards, snakes, turtles, and crocodiles are reptiles. Frogs, toads, and salamanders are amphibians. Both amphibians and reptiles are cold-blooded, which means that the warmth of their bodies depends on their surroundings. Most reptiles and amphibians lay eggs instead of giving birth to their young. Reptiles lay hard-shelled eggs on land, but amphibians lay soft-shelled eggs in the water. When reptiles hatch, they look like tiny adults. Amphibian babies, such as tadpoles or baby frogs, must live underwater until they are older. Adult amphibians spend part of their time in the water and part on land. Reptiles feel dry and scaly to the touch, and amphibians feel moist and sticky. Because amphibians can live both in water and on land, they are more at risk for becoming sick from pollution. It is important to keep ponds and lakes clean so that the animals that live there will be safe and healthy.

12. What is the main idea of this passage?

    a. There are important differences between reptiles and amphibians.

    b. Reptiles are the same as amphibians.

    c. Frogs and lizards belong to different families.

13. Name three animals that are reptiles and three that are amphibians. _____

    _____

    _____

14. The author organizes this passage as a comparison. Why does this organizational pattern work well for this subject?

    _____

FITNESS FLASH: Do arm circles for 30 seconds.

* See page ii.

PLACE STICKER HERE

A student recorded the weight of potatoes she used for a science fair project. Read the data. For each potato, draw an X above the line plot to show its weight.

Potato	A	B	C	D	E	F	G	H	I	J
Weight in pounds	$\frac{3}{4}$	$\frac{1}{4}$	$\frac{2}{4}$	$\frac{3}{4}$	$\frac{1}{4}$	$\frac{2}{4}$	$\frac{1}{4}$	$\frac{2}{4}$	$\frac{4}{4}$	$\frac{1}{4}$

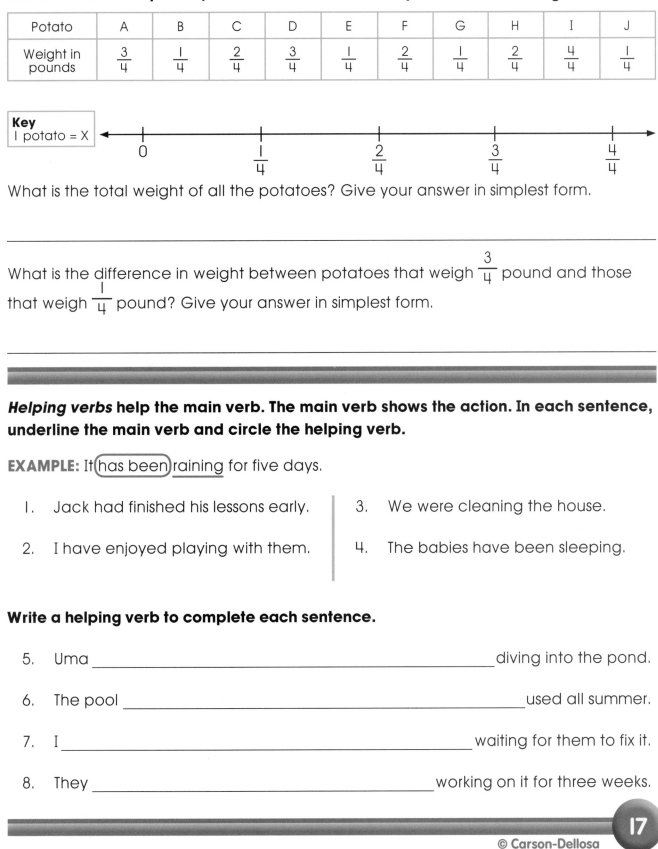

Key
I potato = X

0    $\frac{1}{4}$ $\frac{2}{4}$ $\frac{3}{4}$ $\frac{4}{4}$

What is the total weight of all the potatoes? Give your answer in simplest form.

_____

What is the difference in weight between potatoes that weigh $\frac{3}{4}$ pound and those that weigh $\frac{1}{4}$ pound? Give your answer in simplest form.

_____

Helping verbs **help the main verb. The main verb shows the action. In each sentence, underline the main verb and circle the helping verb.**

EXAMPLE: It (has been) raining for five days.

1. Jack had finished his lessons early.

2. I have enjoyed playing with them.

3. We were cleaning the house.

4. The babies have been sleeping.

Write a helping verb to complete each sentence.

5. Uma _____ diving into the pond.

6. The pool _____ used all summer.

7. I _____ waiting for them to fix it.

8. They _____ working on it for three weeks.

DAY 8

A prefix is added to the beginning of a base word. Add a prefix to the base word in each sentence.

9. The _____ game practice always comes before the game.

10. Do you agree or _____ agree with what I said?

11. Mother is going to _____ arrange the room one more time.

12. The three connected lines make a _____ angle.

13. Everyone on the team wears the same _____ form to the game.

14. You can count on me to _____ pay the money I borrowed.

15. He has to _____ tie his shoelaces to take off his shoes.

16. A _____ cycle has two wheels.

A *metaphor* is a comparison between two objects that does not use the words *like* or *as*. Metaphors can make your writing more descriptive.

EXAMPLE: Mika is a fish in the swimming pool. **Mika swims well.**

Read the sentences. Then, write what each metaphor means.

17. Your smile is a ray of sunshine. _____

18. Winning the award was a dream come true. _____

19. This store is a maze to walk through. _____

20. My pillow was a fluffy cloud. _____

FACTOID: Global temperatures have risen 1.4°F (0.8°C) since 1880.

PLACE STICKER HERE

Solve each word problem.

1. Cammie has 3 coins worth 11¢. What are the coins?

   _____

2. Troy has 7 coins worth 20¢. What are the coins?

   _____

3. Janet has 6 coins worth 47¢. What are the coins?

   _____

4. Jake has 4 coins worth 45¢. What are the coins?

   _____

5. Frankie has 5 coins worth 17¢. What are the coins?

   _____

6. Gary has 6 coins worth 40¢. What are the coins?

   _____

Fill in the blank in each sentence with a relative adverb (*where*, *when*, or *why*).

7. Aaron doesn't know the reason _____ Delia is upset with him.

8. This is the farmers' market _____ we bought the fresh eggs.

9. The construction across the street is the reason _____ I woke up this morning.

10. Have you been to the museum _____ they have a giant dinosaur skeleton?

11. I'd love to borrow that book _____ you finish it.

12. This is the house _____ my grandparents lived when I was little.

13. The afternoon _____ we had a picnic was nearly perfect.

14. Please explain _____ you are so late today.

Read the poem. Then, answer the questions.

Now the Noisy Winds Are Still
by Mary Mapes Dodge

Now the noisy winds are still;
April's coming up the hill!
All the spring is in her train,
Led by shining ranks of rain;
Pit, pat, patter, clatter,
Sudden sun, and clatter, patter!—
First the blue, and then the shower;
Bursting bud, and smiling flower;
Brooks set free with tinkling ring;
Birds too full of song to sing;
Crisp old leaves astir with pride,
Where the timid violets hide,—
All things ready with a will,—
April's coming up the hill!

15. *Onomatopoeia* describes a word that sounds like the object or action it refers to. For example, the word *moo* sounds like the noise a cow makes. Find an example of onomatopoeia in the poem. How does it make the poem more interesting?

_____

16 Name one example of personification found in the poem.

_____

17. What rhyme scheme does the poet use? (Use letters, such as ABAB or ABBA, to

describe it.) _____

18. How does the poet feel about the coming of spring? How do you know?

_____

Circle your answer to each question. Then, underline the root.

1. Which word contains a Latin root that means "one"? Underline the root.

   unicorn   perimeter   biceps

2. Which word contains a Greek root that means "earth"? Underline the root.

   erupt   eject   geology

3. Which word contains a Greek root that means "measure"? Underline the root.

   structure   speedometer   hydrogen

4. Which word contains a Latin root that means "water"? Underline the root.

   manuscript   aquarium   zoology

5. Which word contains a Latin root that means "tooth"? Underline the root.

   carnival   bisect   dentistry

6. Which word contains a Latin root that means "to break"? Underline the root.

   interrupt   fracture   telescope

Multiply to find each product. Then, circle any products that are prime numbers.

7. $9 \times 2 =$ _____

8. $1 \times 11 =$ _____

9. $7 \times 9 =$ _____

10. $8 \times 4 =$ _____

11. $4 \times 7 =$ _____

12. $9 \times 9 =$ _____

13. $1 \times 5 =$ _____

14. $8 \times 3 =$ _____

15. $8 \times 5 =$ _____

16. $7 \times 3 =$ _____

17. $3 \times 3 =$ _____

18. $1 \times 2 =$ _____

19. $4 \times 6 =$ _____

20. $6 \times 3 =$ _____

21. $5 \times 5 =$ _____

22. $9 \times 5 =$ _____

23. $6 \times 9 =$ _____

24. $8 \times 7 =$ _____

25. $8 \times 8 =$ _____

26. $7 \times 1 =$ _____

27. $7 \times 7 =$ _____

DAY 10

Friendship Day is the first Sunday in August. Finish each sentence. Then, draw a picture to show what friendship means to you.

Friends should always _____ .

Friends should never _____ .

I am a good friend because _____ .

Complete each sentence with a prepositional phrase.

EXAMPLE: Tyrone received a package in the mail **from his sister**.

28.　At the movies, Ella sat _____ .

29.　After you chop the vegetables, sauté them_____ .

30.　Take the chairlift_____ , and I'll meet you in the lodge.

31.　Lita and her brother went to the game _____ .

32.　The kitten knocked the napkin _____ .

33.　We were _____this morning when Joseph lost his wallet.

34.　Raise your hands _____ , and then touch your toes.

35.　The bird flew _____ , where I knew it would be safe.

PLACE STICKER HERE

Parallel lines never meet. Draw a line that is parallel to each line segment.

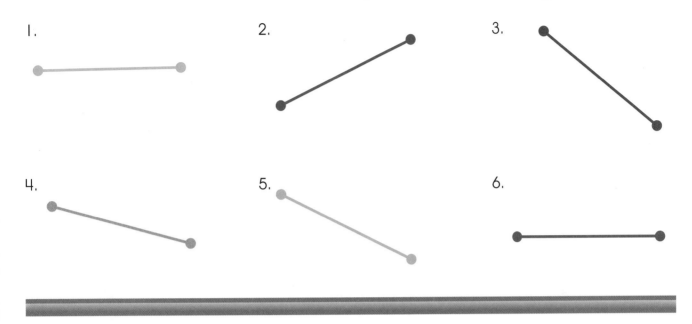

1.

2.

3.

4.

5.

6.

A proper noun starts with a capital letter. Write a proper noun for each common noun.

EXAMPLE: building _____ **White House** _____

7. restaurant_____

8. person _____

9. holiday _____

10. country _____

11. national park_____

12. day_____

13. state_____

14. island _____

15. river_____

16. street _____

Write a common noun for each proper noun.

17. Golden Gate Bridge_____

18. Canada _____

19. San Francisco _____

20. Joseph_____

21. Pacific _____

22. Liberty Bell _____

23. November _____

24. Jamal _____

DAY 11

Solve each problem.

25. 548
     × 5

26. 38
     × 3

27. 1,587
     × 7

28. 2,517
     × 2

29. 3)210

30. 4)526

31. 5)1,839

32. 2)2,548

Separate each run-on sentence into two sentences. Use correct capitalization and punctuation to write the new sentences.

33. Kenya got a haircut she really liked the way it looked.

     _____

     _____

34. The rabbit hopped across the yard it ran into the bushes.

     _____

     _____

35. Molly helped Dad weed the garden then they played in the sprinkler.

     _____

     _____

FACTOID: A shark can grow a new tooth in 24 hours.

PLACE
STICKER
HERE

Add to find each sum.

1.　　　2,456
　　　+ 1,527

2.　　　9,873
　　　+ 1,828

3.　　　18,086
　　　+ 12,302

4.　　　21,421
　　　+ 10,310

5.　　　19,873
　　　+ 1,828

6.　　　8,024
　　　　3,643
　　　+　626

7.　　　4,877
　　　　3,481
　　　+　309

8.　　　5,221
　　　　4,708
　　　+　425

Use a protractor to measure the angle formed by each pair of lines.

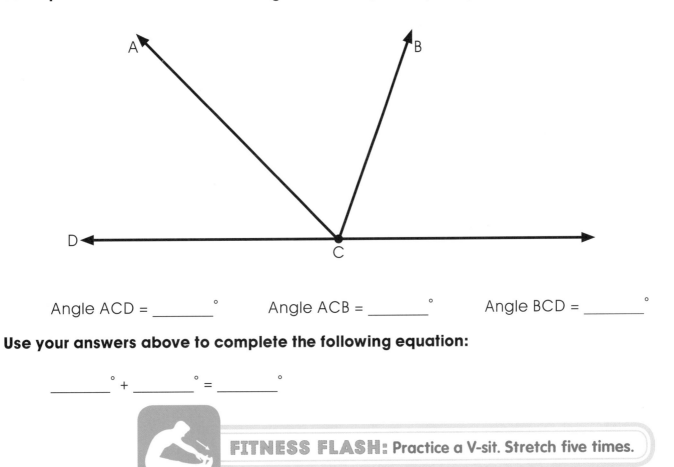

Angle ACD = _____ °　　　Angle ACB = _____ °　　　Angle BCD = _____ °

Use your answers above to complete the following equation:

_____ ° + _____ ° = _____ °

FITNESS FLASH: Practice a V-sit. Stretch five times.

* See page ii.

DAY 12

Write >, <, or = to compare each pair of numbers. Circle the letter next to the greater number. If the numbers are equal, circle both letters. To solve the riddle, write the circled letters in order on the lines.

9. **T** 759 ◯ 258 **S**   10. **H** 161 ◯ 161 **E**

11. **B** 25 ◯ 29 **Y**   12. **B** 230 ◯ 320 **A**

13. **R** 685 ◯ 594 **M**   14. **E** 267 ◯ 267 **S**

15. **M** 141 ◯ 139 **B**   16. **A** 342 ◯ 324 **B**

17. **M** 573 ◯ 753 **R**   18. **L** 206 ◯ 208 **T**

19. **K** 882 ◯ 822 **D**   20. **I** 425 ◯ 254 **S**

21. **A** 330 ◯ 338 **D**   22. **N** 980 ◯ 995 **S**

Why do baby goats know how to compare numbers?

BECAUSE __ __ __ __   __ __ __   __ __ __ __ __   " __ __ __ __ "!

Write a word from the box to identify each figure. Each word will be used once.

perpendicular lines	line	parallel lines	line segment
	point	ray	

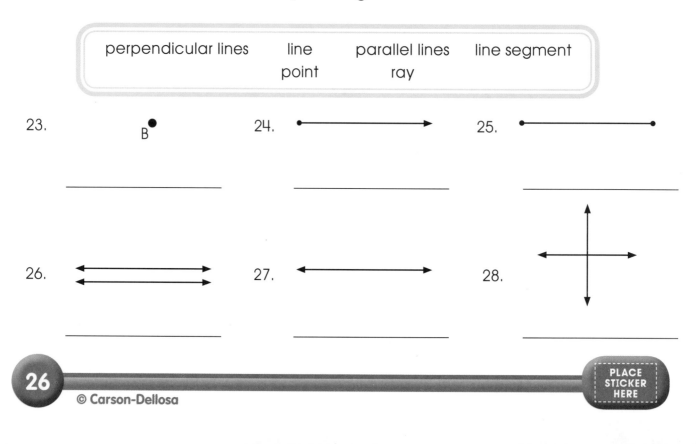

23.   24.   25.

_____   _____   _____

26.   27.   28.

_____   _____   _____

PLACE STICKER HERE

Respect means having consideration for someone else's feelings, possessions, and ideas. By now, you have had many opportunities to learn and show respect. Show your understanding of this key character trait by writing a story for younger children that demonstrates respect. Use a personal example from when you were younger and were learning about respect. After writing your story, design a cover to enclose the pages. Share your story with a younger family member or a family friend to help her learn about this important character trait. Use the space below to plan your story.

_____

_____

_____

_____

_____

Write numbers to tell how many pairs of parallel sides and perpendicular sides each shape has. (Your answer may sometimes be 0.)

1. trapezoid

   pairs of parallel sides: _____

   pairs of perpendicular sides: _____

2. square

   pairs of parallel sides: _____

   pairs of perpendicular sides: _____

3. rhombus

   pairs of parallel sides: _____

   pairs of perpendicular sides: _____

4. right triangle

   pairs of parallel sides: _____

   pairs of perpendicular sides: _____

Read the passage. Then, answer the questions.

Democracy

Democracy is a form of government in which people vote for the leaders who govern them. *Democracy* is derived from a Greek word meaning "popular government." Here, the word *popular* means "of the people" rather than "well liked." The word was first used to describe the political system of Greek city-states, like Athens, in the fourth and fifth centuries BC. In a direct democracy, the people vote on every decision. An example of a direct democracy is a club in which all members vote on decisions such as a poster design or how to raise money. It is hard for large groups to have a direct democracy, so many places, including the United States and Canada, have a representative democracy. In a representative democracy, people elect leaders who vote on the issues. The people trust that their elected leaders will represent their viewpoints. If the people feel that their elected leaders do not represent their viewpoints, then they can vote them out of office.

5.   What is the main idea of this passage?

a.   Democracy is a form of government in which people make the decisions.

b.   An early form of democracy was practiced in Greece.

c.   The United States and Canada both have democratic governments.

6.   What does the Greek word for *democracy* mean?_____

_____

7.   What happens in a direct democracy?_____

_____

8.   What happens in a representative democracy? _____

_____

FACTOID: The largest frog in the world is the goliath frog, which can grow to a length of about one foot (about 30 cm).

PLACE STICKER HERE

Write the correct spelling of each word. If you are unsure, check the spelling in an online or print dictionary.

1. antonim antonym _____

2. mountain mountin _____

3. approximate approximet _____

4. reknewable renewable _____

5. beleive believe _____

6. tutor tuter _____

Shade the models to help solve each equation.

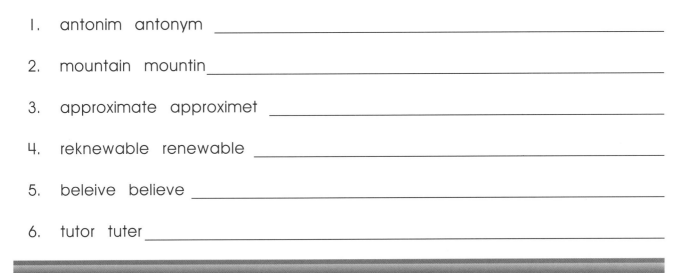

7.

$\frac{5}{8} + \frac{2}{8} =$ _____

8.

$\frac{4}{7} + \frac{1}{7} =$ _____

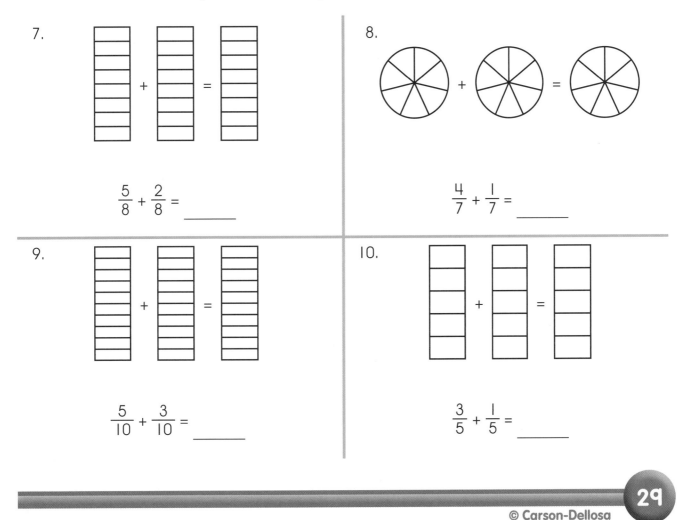

9.

$\frac{5}{10} + \frac{3}{10} =$ _____

10.

$\frac{3}{5} + \frac{1}{5} =$ _____

DAY 14

Measure the length of each side to find the perimeter or the area in centimeters.

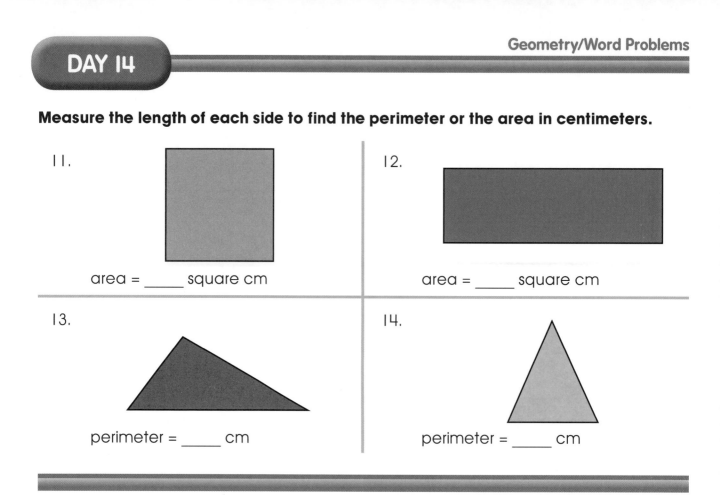

11.

area = _____ square cm

12.

area = _____ square cm

13.

perimeter = _____ cm

14.

perimeter = _____ cm

Solve each word problem. Show your work. Give answers in simplest form.

15. Nola spends 2 hours at the library. She spends $\frac{3}{4}$ of an hour on the computer, $\frac{1}{4}$ of an hour looking for books, and $\frac{1}{4}$ of an hour looking at DVDs. How much time does she have left for reading?

   _____

16. Juan rode his bike $\frac{2}{3}$ mile to school, $\frac{1}{3}$ mile to the library, and $\frac{2}{3}$ mile home. How far did he ride altogether?

   _____

17. William placed a $\frac{5}{8}$-pound weight on a scale. Then, he added four $\frac{1}{8}$-pound weights onto the scale. What is the total weight on the scale?

   _____

18. Gwen had a bag of cashews. She gave $\frac{3}{16}$ of the cashews to her sister and ate another $\frac{7}{16}$. What fraction of the cashews is left?

   _____

Subtract to find each difference.

1.   4,314
    − 2,532
	2. 3,826
	    − 49
		3. 2,182
		    − 396
			4. 5,433
			    − 25

5.   6,922
    − 5,833
	6. 22,318
	    − 17,725
		7. 57,260
		    − 23,458
			8. 68,011
			    − 14,343

Is the line drawn on each figure a line of symmetry? Write *yes* or *no*.

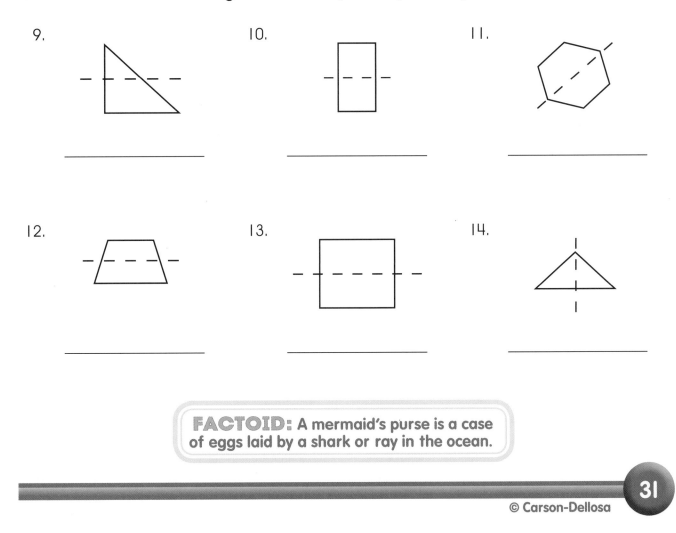

9.

10.

11.

_____

_____

_____

12.

13.

14.

_____

_____

_____

DAY 15

Solve each problem. Write the answer in simplest form.

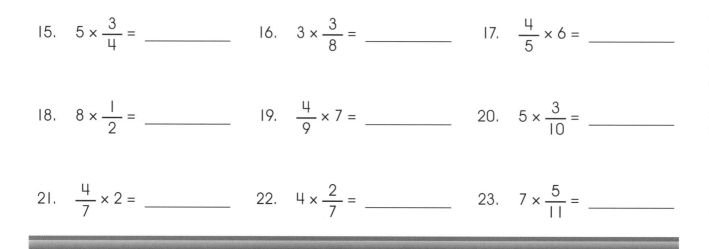

15. $5 \times \dfrac{3}{4} =$ _____

16. $3 \times \dfrac{3}{8} =$ _____

17. $\dfrac{4}{5} \times 6 =$ _____

18. $8 \times \dfrac{1}{2} =$ _____

19. $\dfrac{4}{9} \times 7 =$ _____

20. $5 \times \dfrac{3}{10} =$ _____

21. $\dfrac{4}{7} \times 2 =$ _____

22. $4 \times \dfrac{2}{7} =$ _____

23. $7 \times \dfrac{5}{11} =$ _____

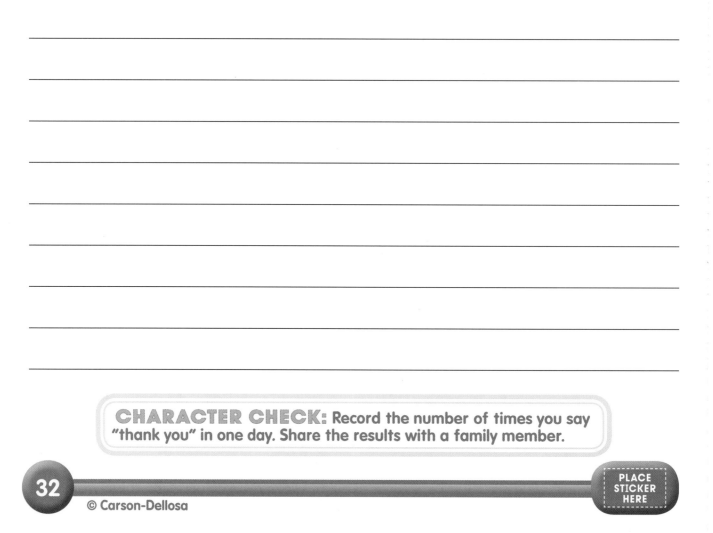

Charlie's parents have just told him that their family will be moving across the country in a month. Write a short story about Charlie's reaction to the news. Use dialogue in your writing.

_____

_____

_____

_____

_____

_____

_____

_____

CHARACTER CHECK: Record the number of times you say "thank you" in one day. Share the results with a family member.

PLACE STICKER HERE

Draw a line through the word that does not belong in each sentence.

1. All of the butterflies will be gone went by October.

2. The state vegetable of Idaho is are the potato.

3. She will hid hide behind the large, old tree.

4. I have ridden rode my horse regularly this summer.

5. Our dog constantly goes to that corner to dig digging.

In each problem, change the fraction with a denominator of 10 to an equivalent fraction with a denominator of 100. Then, add.

6. $\dfrac{2}{10} + \dfrac{5}{100} =$ _____

7. $\dfrac{3}{10} + \dfrac{25}{100} =$ _____

8. $\dfrac{72}{100} + \dfrac{2}{10} =$ _____

9. $\dfrac{1}{10} + \dfrac{40}{100} =$ _____

10. $\dfrac{13}{100} + \dfrac{8}{10} =$ _____

11. $\dfrac{5}{10} + \dfrac{45}{100} =$ _____

12. $\dfrac{2}{10} + \dfrac{17}{100} =$ _____

13. $\dfrac{75}{100} + \dfrac{1}{10} =$ _____

14. $\dfrac{3}{10} + \dfrac{44}{100} =$ _____

15. $\dfrac{34}{100} + \dfrac{1}{10} =$ _____

16. $\dfrac{4}{10} + \dfrac{32}{100} =$ _____

17. $\dfrac{2}{10} + \dfrac{16}{100} =$ _____

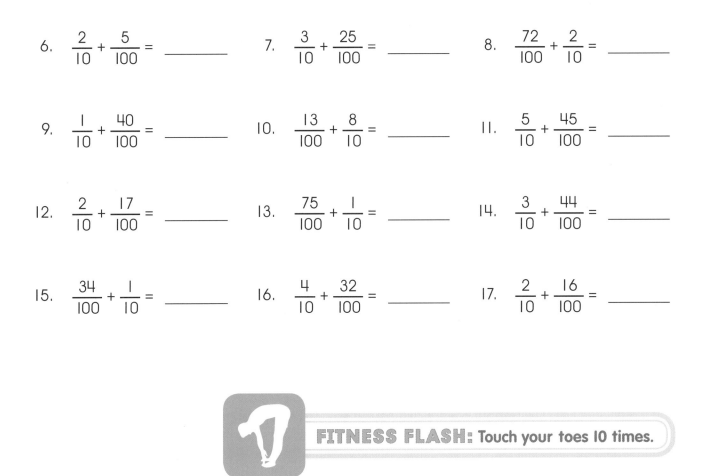

FITNESS FLASH: Touch your toes 10 times.

* See page ii.

DAY 16

Solve each problem.

18.   7,548
      − 3,762

19.   8,562
      + 2,163

20.   5,585
      − 2,609

21.   36,814
     − 7,523

22.   53,397
   + 39,288

23.   3,245
      5,029
     + 6,981

24.   9,421
      8,389
     + 4,506

25.   3,340
      7,189
     + 4,482

Compare the decimals in each pair. Use the greater than (>), less than (<), or equal to (=) symbols.

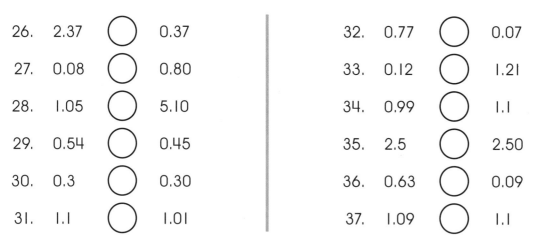

26. 2.37 ◯ 0.37

27. 0.08 ◯ 0.80

28. 1.05 ◯ 5.10

29. 0.54 ◯ 0.45

30. 0.3 ◯ 0.30

31. 1.1 ◯ 1.01

32. 0.77 ◯ 0.07

33. 0.12 ◯ 1.21

34. 0.99 ◯ 1.1

35. 2.5 ◯ 2.50

36. 0.63 ◯ 0.09

37. 1.09 ◯ 1.1

FACTOID: Manhole covers are round so that they can't fall into the manholes.

PLACE
STICKER
HERE

Replace each word in parentheses with a synonym.

EXAMPLE: The man (said) _____**yelled**_____ , "Watch out for that bee!"

1. Margaret (said) _____ , "Please come to my party."

2. Mother always (said) _____ , "A stitch in time saves nine."

3. "Is it already time to leave?" (said) _____ Casey.

4. "I don't like celery in soup," (said) _____ Dad.

5. "My kite is still in the air," (said) _____ Tony.

6. The boy with his mouth full of noodles (said) _____
    that he wanted more.

Every dictionary page has guide words at the top. They tell the first word on the page and the last word on the page. Write each word in alphabetical order under the correct guide words.

| aggravate | aboard | about | aid | ailment |
| above | affect | after | agree | afford |

7. aardvark • afghan

8. Africa • aim

_____

_____

_____

_____

DAY 17

Read the passage. Then, answer the questions.

Arachne the Weaver

Long ago in Greece, there lived a young girl whose name was Arachne. All she cared to do from morning until night was to spin and weave. And oh, how fine were the things she wove! One day, a stranger appeared by her side and asked, "Did Athena, queen of the air, teach you to spin and weave so well?"

"Can she weave goods like mine? I should like to see her try!" Arachne **scoffed**. She looked up and saw a woman wrapped in a long cloak.

"I am the goddess Athena," said the woman, "and I have heard your boast. Do you think you can spin and weave as well as I?"

"Yes," replied Arachne.

"Then we shall have a contest," said Athena. "If your work is best, then I will weave no more. But if my work is best, then you shall never use a loom again."

The two women set to weaving. Arachne was soon ashamed when she saw the beauty of Athena's work. "How can I live," she cried, "now that I may never spin again?" Athena took pity on the girl. She changed Arachne into a nimble spider. Ever since that day, spiders keep busy from morning until night, weaving beautiful webs.

9. An *origin myth* explains how something came to be. What does this origin myth

    explain? _____

10. How are Arachne and Athena similar? How are they different?

    _____

11. What does the word *scoffed* mean in the story?

    _____

12. The story of Arachne is a Greek myth. Find another example of a Greek myth.
    What similarities does it have to the story of Arachne?

    _____

PLACE
STICKER
HERE

Circle the greater measurement.

1.	13 cm	13 mm
2.	36 in.	36 yd.
3.	10 cups	10 oz.
4.	12 km	12 m
5.	25 kg	25 g
6.	2 tons	2,000 lbs.

7.	14 mL	14 L
8.	5,000 ft.	5 mi.
9.	14 gal.	14 qt.
10.	100 cm	10 m
11.	25 lbs.	250 oz.
12.	80 mm	800 cm

Write two sentences using the word _it's_ and two sentences using the word _its_.

EXAMPLE: It's very hot outside today.

That shoe has lost its shoelaces.

13. _____

14. _____

15. _____

16. _____

Write two sentences using the word _eight_ and two sentences using the word _ate_.

17. _____

18. _____

19. _____

20. _____

CHARACTER CHECK: Look up the word _considerate_ in a dictionary. Then, think of two ways that you can be considerate.

DAY 18

Write a story about taking a trip to outer space. Tell what kinds of things you should pack and how you should prepare. Describe where you would like to go and what you think it would be like there.

_____

_____

_____

_____

_____

_____

_____

_____

_____

_____

_____

_____

_____

_____

FACTOID: You consume one-tenth of a calorie every time you lick a stamp.

PLACE STICKER HERE

Read the passage. Then, answer the questions.

Nutrition

The food you eat helps your body grow. It gives you energy to work and play. Eating a variety of good foods each day will help you stay healthy. What you eat and how much food you need depend on whether you are a girl or a boy, how active you are, and your age. To find out what foods you should eat and how much food you need, go to *www.choosemyplate.gov/kids/* and download the SuperTracker tool.

1. Why should you eat a variety of foods? _____

2. What are some things that can affect how much food you need? _____

3. From which food group did you eat the least today? _____

4. Which of your meals included the most food groups today? _____

Circle each noun that should begin with a capital letter.

5. My friends emmett and hugo want to join the boy scouts.

6. When his family was in idaho, rashad floated down snake river.

7. Does your cousin sierra go to winn elementary school?

8. Last night, doug stopped at brookstown mall to buy a gift.

9. I heard that ms. hernandez's class visited the lincoln memorial in washington, d.c.

10. Have you ever visited niagara falls in canada?

DAY 19

Solve each word problem.

11. Jennifer bought a bag of apples for $2.50. The tax was 19¢. She used a coupon for 42¢ off. How much did she pay?

12. Bradley bought a shirt for $5 off the original price of $24. The tax was $1.40. How much did Bradley pay?

13. Elise has a job baby-sitting. She worked 4 hours on Wednesday and 5 hours on Friday. She earns $5 an hour. How much did she earn?

14. Gayle had $38. After she bought 5 containers of detergent, she had $3 left. How much was each container of detergent?

Draw a line to connect each word to its meaning.

EXAMPLE:

honorable   a kind of lamp

15. current   to make clearly known

16. knowledge   having a good reputation

17. suspicion   occupation, source of livelihood

18. exact   leaving no room for error, accurate

19. lantern   now in progress

20. profession   information, awareness, understanding

21. universal   worldwide, understood by all

22. agriculture   the science and art of farming

23. declare   doubt

FITNESS FLASH: Do 10 shoulder shrugs.

* See page ii.

PLACE STICKER HERE

Convert each improper fraction to a mixed number.

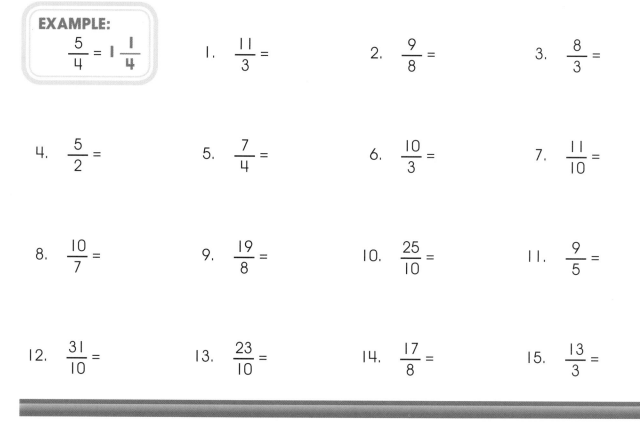

EXAMPLE:

$$\frac{5}{4} = 1\frac{1}{4}$$

1. $\frac{11}{3} =$

2. $\frac{9}{8} =$

3. $\frac{8}{3} =$

4. $\frac{5}{2} =$

5. $\frac{7}{4} =$

6. $\frac{10}{3} =$

7. $\frac{11}{10} =$

8. $\frac{10}{7} =$

9. $\frac{19}{8} =$

10. $\frac{25}{10} =$

11. $\frac{9}{5} =$

12. $\frac{31}{10} =$

13. $\frac{23}{10} =$

14. $\frac{17}{8} =$

15. $\frac{13}{3} =$

The Continental Congress adopted the first official American flag on June 14, 1777. The American flag was a symbol of unity for the beginning nation.

Design and draw your own flag. Then, write a paragraph on a separate sheet of paper explaining what your flag symbolizes. What do the colors mean? What do the images represent?

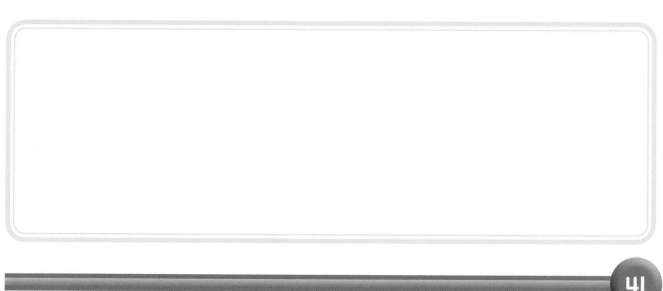

You can use this Activity Pyramid to help plan your summer exercise program. Fill in each blank.

16. List one thing that is not good exercise that you could omit from your summer program.

a. _____

17. List three exercises that you could do to build strength and flexibility.

a. _____

b. _____

c. _____

18. List two sports in which you would like to participate.

a. _____

b. _____

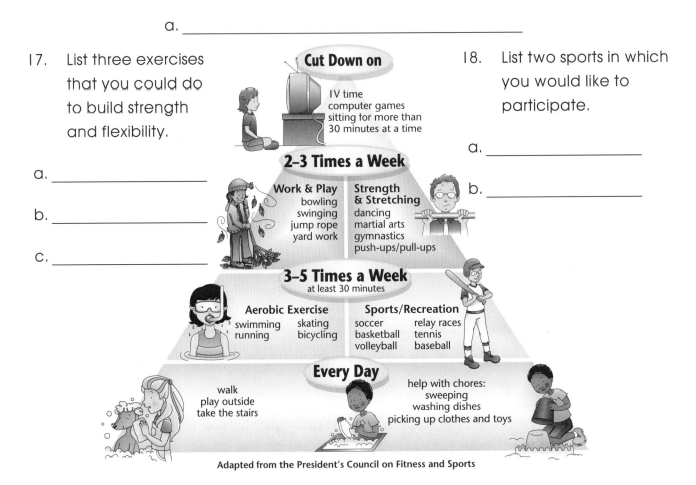

Cut Down on
IV time
computer games
sitting for more than
30 minutes at a time

2–3 Times a Week

Work & Play
bowling
swinging
jump rope
yard work

Strength & Stretching
dancing
martial arts
gymnastics
push-ups/pull-ups

3–5 Times a Week
at least 30 minutes

Aerobic Exercise
swimming   skating
running   bicycling

Sports/Recreation
soccer   relay races
basketball tennis
volleyball baseball

Every Day

walk
play outside
take the stairs

help with chores:
sweeping
washing dishes
picking up clothes and toys

Adapted from the President's Council on Fitness and Sports

List three everyday things that you could do to get moving more often.

19. _____

20. _____

21. _____

CHARACTER CHECK: Draw a picture of yourself with your best friend. Show your picture to an adult and explain why you like being friends with this person.

* See page ii.

42

PLACE STICKER HERE

Determining Your Heart Rate

Your heart is one of the most important organs in your body because it helps all of the other organs work. It is important to keep your heart pumping at a healthy rate. So, how do you know how fast your heart is pumping?

Materials:

- stopwatch or watch with a second hand

Procedure:

1. Place your index and middle fingers just under your jaw where it meets your neck. You should feel your heartbeat. A large artery that supplies blood to your brain is located there. Count the number of heartbeats for six seconds. Multiply that number by 10 to determine your heart rate. Record your heart rate on the table below.

2. Now, measure how fast your heart beats after certain activities. Complete the table to track your results. Do each activity for one minute. Then, measure your heart rate using the six-second count.

Activity	Number of beats in six seconds	Heartbeats per minute (multiply by 10)
Resting		
Running in place		
Jumping jacks		
Push-ups		

Conclusion:

Your heart pumps blood, oxygen, and energy to your entire body. The more you exercise, the faster your heart needs to pump. That is why activities like running in place make your heart beat faster than it beats while resting. Running takes more energy than resting.

Continue this experiment with other activities. What increases your heart rate the most? The least? How do you feel when your heart is beating faster?

BONUS

Build a Backbone

Where would you be without a backbone? You would not be able to walk. You would not even be able to sit in a chair! The backbone is an amazing structure. Without it, you would not be able to do much of anything! Build a model backbone to see just how important it is.

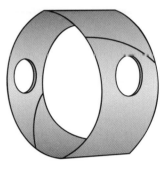

Materials:

- 11 cardboard tubes (short)
- Hole punch
- 11 rubber bands (2" or about 5 cm long)
- Scissors

Procedure:

1. Carefully cut each cardboard tube into thirds.
2. Punch two holes on opposite sides of each tube.
3. Loop the rubber bands together to form one long string. Thread the string of rubber bands through the holes in the tube sections, one at a time. When all of the sections are threaded on the rubber band string, tie off the string at the top and bottom.
4. Now, experiment with your model backbone. Bend it in different directions to see if it has any limitations. Try to figure out what would happen if one or more of the sections were damaged or had to be removed.

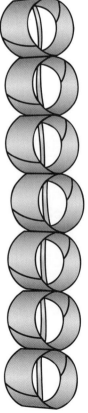

Conclusion:

The backbone serves as the major supporting structure in the body, which means it must possess a lot of rigidity. At the same time, it must be flexible to allow twisting, turning, and bending. The human spine has 33 vertebrae. They allow swaying and bending and, at the same time, provide support for the head and a place for the ribs and the pelvis to attach.

Research pictures of different animal vertebrae. How do your vertebrae compare to the vertebrae of a giraffe? How do they compare to the vertebrae of a snake?

A Famous Place

Research a famous world landmark. Take notes on the lines below. Then, design an advertisement that encourages travelers to visit that landmark. Include information about the landmark's location and interesting facts about its history.

_____

_____

_____

BONUS

The Iditarod®

The Iditarod® is a dogsled race through Alaska. The chart below gives approximate distances between checkpoints along the race. Using the scale **1 inch = 5 miles (8 km)**, determine how many lengths of the scale would be needed to show each distance on a map. Write your answers in the blanks below.

Checkpoints	Distance between Checkpoints
Kaltag to Unalakleet	90 miles (144.8 km)
Unalakleet to Shaktoolik	40 miles (64.4 km)
Shaktoolik to Koyuk	50 miles (80.5 km)
Koyuk to Elim	50 miles (80.5 km)
Elim to Golovin	30 miles (48.3 km)
Golovin to White Mountain	20 miles (32.2 km)
White Mountain to Safety	55 miles (88.5 km)
Safety to Nome	20 miles (32.2 km)

		Miles	**Number of Lengths of 1-inch scale**
1.	White Mountain to Safety	_____	_____
2.	Koyuk to Elim	_____	_____
3.	Safety to Nome	_____	_____
4.	Unalakleet to Shaktoolik	_____	_____
5.	Elim to Golovin	_____	_____
6.	Golovin to White Mountain	_____	_____
7.	Kaltag to Unalakleet	_____	_____
8.	Shaktoolik to Koyuk	_____	_____

Time Zones

This map shows the time zones in the United States. Use this time zone map to answer each question.

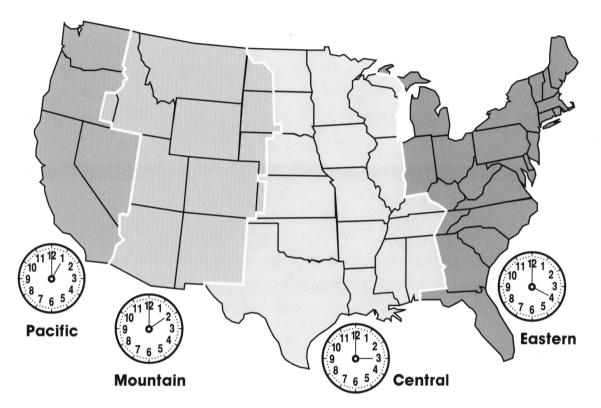

1. If it is 2:00 P.M. in Washington, D.C., what time is it in Alabama? _____

2. If it is noon in California, what time is it in Wyoming? _____

3. If it is 9:00 A.M. in Montana, what time is it in Iowa? _____

4. If it is 6:00 P.M. in North Carolina, what time is it in Arizona? _____

5. If it is 1:00 P.M. in Maine, what time is it in Nevada? _____

BONUS

Take It Outside!

By the time summer arrives, insects are very active. Take advantage of this time to observe a variety of insects. Fireflies, ants, and ladybugs and other beetles will provide you with many learning opportunities. Examine the insects and their habits. Look at what they eat and how they move. Make sure you do not touch or disturb the insects. Keep a journal to write your observations. Visit a library to find several books about the insects you studied. Read the books and compare the information you observed with what you read. Share what you learn with a friend or family member.

With an adult, go for a walk outside with a camera. Take a variety of pictures that make you think of summer, such as fireflies glowing in the late evening. After printing the pictures, look for similarities and differences and place the pictures into groups. Determine various percentages based on your groupings, such as what percent of the pictures contained water. Graph your results.

Summer is the perfect time of year to find a variety of healthful foods because many crops are harvested in the summer. With an adult, arrange to visit a local farmers' market, a plant nursery, or a garden supply store. Find out which foods grow best in your area. Talk to local farmers, gardeners, and grocers to learn about the importance of eating locally grown foods. Encourage your family to buy and eat those delicious, healthful foods.

* See page ii.

Monthly Goals

Think of three goals to set for yourself this month. For example, you may want to exercise for 30 minutes each day. Write your goals on the lines and review them with an adult.

Place a sticker next to each goal that you complete. Feel proud that you have met your goals!

1. _____ PLACE STICKER HERE

2. _____ PLACE STICKER HERE

3. _____ PLACE STICKER HERE

Word List

The following words are used in this section. They are good words for you to know. Read each word aloud. Use a dictionary to look up each word that you do not know. Then, write two sentences. Use a word from the word list in each sentence.

community	opinion
fraction	procedure
furrowed	traditional
material	transportation

1. _____

_____

2. _____

_____

Introduction to Strength

This section includes fitness and character development activities that focus on strength. These activities are designed to get you moving and thinking about strengthening your body and your character.

Physical Strength

Like flexibility, strength is necessary for you to be healthy. You may think that a strong person is someone who can lift a lot of weight. However, strength is more than the ability to pick up heavy things. Strength is built over time. You are stronger now than you were in preschool. What are some activities that you can do now that you could not do then?

You can gain strength through everyday activities and many fun exercises. Carry grocery bags to build your arms. Ride a bike to strengthen your legs. Swim to strengthen your whole body. Exercises such as push-ups and chin-ups are also great strength builders.

Set goals this summer to improve your strength. Base your goals on activities you enjoy. Talk about your goals with an adult. As you meet your goals, set new ones. Celebrate your stronger, healthier body!

Strength of Character

As you build your physical strength, work on your inner strength, too. Having a strong character means standing up for who you are, even if others do not agree with your point of view.

You can show inner strength in many ways, such as being honest, supporting someone who needs your help, and putting your best efforts into every task. It is not always easy to show inner strength. Can you think of a time when you used inner strength to handle a situation, such as being teased by another child at the park?

Improve your inner strength over the summer. Think about ways you can show strength of character, such as having good sportsmanship in your baseball league. Reflect on your positive growth. Be proud of your strong character!

Triceps Dip

Have an adult help you complete dips to strengthen your triceps, the muscles in the back of your arms. Find a sturdy chair or bench. If using a chair, have an adult hold the back of the chair for balance. Face away from the chair. Place both hands on the edge of the seat. Extend your legs so that you are holding yourself up with your arms. Lower your body until your upper arms are parallel to the seat. Then, push yourself up. Repeat several times to see how many dips you can complete. Try this activity several times each week. Keep track of your progress over the summer.

A prefix is added to the beginning of a base word. A suffix is added to the end of a base word. Add the prefix *mis-*, *un-*, or *re-* to each word. Then, write a sentence using the whole word.

1. _____lucky _____

2. _____judge _____

3. _____spell _____

4. _____fill _____

5. _____build _____

Add the suffix *-er*, *-less*, *-ful*, or *-ed* to each word. Then, write a sentence using the whole word.

6. use _____ _____

7. spell _____ _____

* See page ii.

An *opinion* is a belief or viewpoint that is not based on fact. You probably have many opinions about things, such as the best flavor of ice cream or which animal makes the best pet. People may be more willing to listen to and agree with your opinions if you state them clearly and persuasively. On a separate sheet of paper, write a three-paragraph persuasive essay on one of the topics provided.

1. People should always wear seat belts.
2. Children should be able to eat whatever they want.
3. Students should never have to do homework.
4. We should help people in other countries.

_____

_____

_____

_____

_____

_____

_____

_____

_____

_____

_____

FACTOID: No word in the English language rhymes with *film, gulf,* or *wolf.*

PLACE STICKER HERE

Multiply to find each product.

1.	12	2.	12	3.	22	4.	18	5.	23
	× 6		× 4		× 6		× 2		× 4

6.	23	7.	34	8.	16	9.	78	10.	86
	× 7		× 6		× 5		× 5		× 7

Read each sentence. If it is a complete sentence, write *C* on the line. If it is a fragment, write *F*, and if it is a run-on, write *R*. Then, choose one fragment and one run-on to rewrite correctly on the long lines.

11. _____ Went to the YMCA on Friday afternoon.

12. _____ Maya's favorite subject is science because she likes doing experiments.

13. _____ Bryson went to the waterpark on Saturday he went to the library on Sunday.

14. _____ Lakesia volunteers at the animal shelter with her aunt.

15. _____ After school, the students met in the cafeteria they wanted to plan the school dance.

16. _____ Forgot the permission slip for the field trip.

_____

_____

FITNESS FLASH: Do 10 lunges.

* See page ii.

DAY 2

Complete each table.

17. 5 pennies = 1 nickel

pennies	5	10	15	20	25	30
nickels	1					

18. 10 dimes = 1 dollar

dimes	10	20	30			
dollars	1	2				

19. 6 cans of juice = 1 carton

cans	6	12		24		36
cartons	1		3		5	

Divide to find each quotient.

EXAMPLE:

$$\begin{array}{r} 2\ R8 \\ 20\overline{)48} \\ -40 \\ \hline 8 \end{array}$$

20. $30\overline{)189}$

21. $70\overline{)456}$

22. $80\overline{)504}$

23. $30\overline{)281}$

24. $60\overline{)246}$

25. $90\overline{)458}$

26. $60\overline{)573}$

27. $40\overline{)172}$

When a whole object is divided into 100 equal parts, each part is one hundredth ($\frac{1}{100}$ or 0.01). Write each fraction as a decimal.

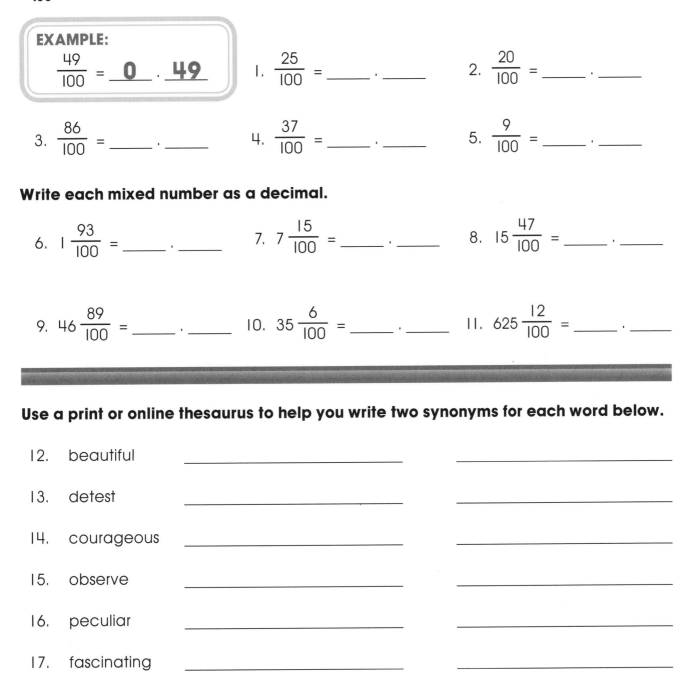

EXAMPLE:

$\frac{49}{100}$ = **0** . **49**

1. $\frac{25}{100}$ = _____ . _____

2. $\frac{20}{100}$ = _____ . _____

3. $\frac{86}{100}$ = _____ . _____

4. $\frac{37}{100}$ = _____ . _____

5. $\frac{9}{100}$ = _____ . _____

Write each mixed number as a decimal.

6. $1\frac{93}{100}$ = _____ . _____

7. $7\frac{15}{100}$ = _____ . _____

8. $15\frac{47}{100}$ = _____ . _____

9. $46\frac{89}{100}$ = _____ . _____

10. $35\frac{6}{100}$ = _____ . _____

11. $625\frac{12}{100}$ = _____ . _____

Use a print or online thesaurus to help you write two synonyms for each word below.

12. beautiful _____ _____

13. detest _____ _____

14. courageous _____ _____

15. observe _____ _____

16. peculiar _____ _____

17. fascinating _____ _____

DAY 3

Write >, <, or = to compare each pair of fractions. Use the fraction table for help.

18. $\frac{1}{2} \bigcirc \frac{1}{4}$ 19. $\frac{2}{3} \bigcirc \frac{1}{3}$

20. $\frac{1}{4} \bigcirc \frac{1}{6}$ 21. $\frac{2}{6} \bigcirc \frac{1}{3}$

22. $\frac{4}{8} \bigcirc \frac{2}{10}$ 23. $\frac{1}{12} \bigcirc \frac{1}{10}$

24. $\frac{3}{4} \bigcirc \frac{2}{8}$ 25. $\frac{2}{5} \bigcirc \frac{1}{3}$

26. $\frac{3}{8} \bigcirc \frac{10}{12}$ 27. $\frac{2}{8} \bigcirc \frac{1}{4}$

28. $\frac{1}{5} \bigcirc \frac{2}{10}$ 29. $\frac{1}{3} \bigcirc \frac{2}{4}$

$\frac{1}{2}$				$\frac{1}{2}$		
$\frac{1}{3}$		$\frac{1}{3}$			$\frac{1}{3}$	
$\frac{1}{4}$		$\frac{1}{4}$		$\frac{1}{4}$		$\frac{1}{4}$
$\frac{1}{5}$	$\frac{1}{5}$		$\frac{1}{5}$		$\frac{1}{5}$	$\frac{1}{5}$
$\frac{1}{6}$	$\frac{1}{6}$	$\frac{1}{6}$	$\frac{1}{6}$	$\frac{1}{6}$		$\frac{1}{6}$
$\frac{1}{8}$	$\frac{1}{8}$	$\frac{1}{8}$	$\frac{1}{8}$	$\frac{1}{8}$	$\frac{1}{8}$	$\frac{1}{8}$ $\frac{1}{8}$
$\frac{1}{10}$	$\frac{1}{10}$	$\frac{1}{10}$	$\frac{1}{10}$	$\frac{1}{10}$	$\frac{1}{10}$	$\frac{1}{10}$ $\frac{1}{10}$ $\frac{1}{10}$ $\frac{1}{10}$
$\frac{1}{12}$	$\frac{1}{12}$	$\frac{1}{12}$	$\frac{1}{12}$	$\frac{1}{12}$	$\frac{1}{12}$	$\frac{1}{12}$ $\frac{1}{12}$ $\frac{1}{12}$ $\frac{1}{12}$ $\frac{1}{12}$ $\frac{1}{12}$

Sometimes, informal language is appropriate. Other times, formal language is needed. Read each pair of sentences. Write _I_ next to sentences with informal wording and _F_ next to those with formal wording.

30. _____ It's been a pleasure speaking with you.

_____ Talk to ya soon!

31. _____ This is totally unbelievable, but an anaconda can grow to be a whopping 30 feet!

_____ The anaconda, a South American water snake, can grow to be 30 feet in length.

32. _____ I look forward to seeing you again soon.

_____ Catch you later!

Personification is giving human characteristics to nonhuman things. Use personification to answer each question.

1. What would a pencil say to a hand? _____

_____

2. What would a carpet say to a foot? _____

_____

3. What would a basketball say to a basketball player? _____

_____

4. What would a skateboard say to a skateboarder? _____

_____

Earth already has many different kinds of insects, but there is always room for one more! Create a new insect. Write about what it looks like, where it lives, what it eats, and what predators it must avoid.

_____

_____

_____

_____

_____

_____

_____

_____

DAY 4

Read the passage. Then, answer the questions.

Community Helpers

A community is a group of people who live in the same area or have the same interests. Communities need helpers to make everything function well. Some important community helpers are police officers and firefighters. Police officers make sure that everyone is following the laws of the community to keep people safe. Firefighters put out fires and educate people about fire safety. Other community helpers are people who work for the city, such as trash collectors and park rangers. Trash collectors drive down streets to collect everybody's trash. Park rangers make sure that city parks are clean and safe so that people can play or have picnics in them. Librarians are also important helpers in the community. Librarians make sure that a lot of good books are available in the library for everyone in the community to read. The next time you see a community helper, say, "Thank you!"

5. What is the main idea of this passage?

   a. A community needs a lot of people to make it function well.

   b. Police officers and firefighters are community helpers.

   c. People like to have picnics in city parks.

6. What is the role of police officers in a community? _____

   _____

7. What is the role of firefighters in a community? _____

   _____

8. How does the author support the idea that communities need helpers to make everything function well?

   _____

FITNESS FLASH: Do 10 squats.

* See page ii.

PLACE STICKER HERE

Multiply to find each product.

1. 4 x 10 = _____
2. 600 x 6 = _____
3. 7 x 800 = _____
4. 30 x 8 = _____
5. 5 x 20 = _____
6. 800 x 5 = _____
7. 8 x 90 = _____
8. 50 x 6 = _____
9. 600 x 5 = _____
10. 4 x 100 = _____
11. 7 x 80 = _____
12. 7 x 500 = _____
13. 900 x 7 = _____
14. 600 x 4 = _____
15. 900 x 4 = _____
16. 8 x 900 = _____
17. 800 x 2 = _____
18. 7 x 900 = _____
19. 3 x 10 = _____
20. 700 x 6 = _____
21. 3 x 800 = _____
22. 7 x 40 = _____
23. 9 x 10 = _____
24. 10 x 100 = _____

Use the words in the word bank to complete the proverbs.

bird	grow	crying	saved	right	eggs	boils	well

25. Two wrongs don't make a _____ .

26. It is no use _____ over spilled milk.

27. A watched kettle never _____ .

28. A penny _____ is a penny earned.

29. The early _____ catches the worm.

30. Absence makes the heart _____ fonder.

31. Don't put all your _____ in one basket.

32. If a thing is worth doing, it is worth doing _____ .

Look at the table about trees. Then, answer the questions.

Tree	Bark	Wood	Leaves
Elm	brown and rough	strong	oval shaped, saw-toothed edges, sharp points
Birch	creamy white, peels off in layers	elastic, won't break easily	heart shaped or triangular with pointed tips
Oak	dark gray, thick, rough, deeply furrowed	hard, fine grained	round, finger-shaped lobes
Willow	rough and broken	brown, soft, light	long, narrow, curved at tips
Maple	rough and gray	strong	in pairs, shaped like an open hand
Hickory	loose, peels off	white, hard	shaped like spearheads
Holly	ash colored	hard, fine grained	glossy, sharp tipped

33. Which tree has heart-shaped leaves? _____

34. How many trees have hard wood? _____

35. Which tree has sharp-tipped leaves? _____

36. Which tree has wood like a rubber band? _____

37. What are the different colors of bark? _____

38. From which tree do you think we get syrup? _____

39. Can you identify any of the trees from the table in your yard or your neighborhood? Which ones? _____

CHARACTER CHECK: Why do you think it is important to always be honest?

PLACE STICKER HERE

Complete the multiplication table.

✕	1	10	100	1,000
1	1	10		
2				
3		30		
4				4,000
5				
6				
7			700	
8				
9				9,000

How does multiplying by hundreds differ from multiplying by tens? _____

_____

Write *it's*, *its*, *your*, or *you're* to complete each sentence.

1. I hope that_____ coming to my barn dance.

2. The dance will be for _____ friends also.

3. Do you think _____ too cold for a barn dance?

4. _____ starting time is 8 o'clock.

5. Will _____ family come to the dance with you?

6. _____ floor is long and wide.

FACTOID: Although a polar bear appears white, its skin is black, and its fur is actually made up of clear, hollow tubes.

DAY 6

Read the passage. Then, answer the questions.

World Holidays

The United States celebrates several special holidays every year. People in different countries, however, recognize different holidays. Many people in China celebrate a Lantern Festival to welcome the new year. Special lanterns are lit, and colorful parades march through the streets. In Scotland, some people celebrate Burns Night, which is a holiday in honor of the Scottish poet Robert Burns. Families or club members gather together for a special meal and a reading of Burns's poetry. Whereas the United States celebrates its independence on Independence Day (July 4), Canada celebrates Canada Day on July 1, the date that the government of Canada was created. On both Canada Day and Independence Day, people have community parades, picnics, and fireworks. People in some parts of Germany celebrate Oktoberfest to mark the harvest. They eat traditional German foods like sausages and potato salad. Immigrants brought their native foods and traditions when they left their homelands, so now many celebrate their old holidays in their new countries.

7. What is the main idea of this passage?

    a. Burns Night is a special holiday in Scotland.

    b. People around the world celebrate different holidays.

    c. Oktoberfest takes place in many cities.

8. How do people in Scotland honor Robert Burns? _____

    _____

    _____

9. Research a holiday from a different country that is not mentioned in the passage. Tell what traditions are associated with that holiday.

    _____

    _____

FACTOID: Almonds are in the same family as peaches and roses.

PLACE
STICKER
HERE

To find the product of multiples of 10 or 100, find the product of the basic fact and then count the zeros in the factors. Solve each problem and write how many zeros are in the answer.

$10 \times 8 = 80$ (1 zero) $10 \times 80 = 800$ (2 zeros) $10 \times 800 = 8,000$ (3 zeros)

1. $7 \times 100 =$ _____

2. $39 \times 10 =$ _____

3. $30 \times 300 =$ _____

4.
$$\begin{array}{r} 900 \\ \times\ 40 \\ \hline \end{array}$$

5.
$$\begin{array}{r} 600 \\ \times\ 10 \\ \hline \end{array}$$

6.
$$\begin{array}{r} 230 \\ \times\ 20 \\ \hline \end{array}$$

7.
$$\begin{array}{r} 700 \\ \times\ 80 \\ \hline \end{array}$$

8.
$$\begin{array}{r} 5,000 \\ \times\ \ \ 50 \\ \hline \end{array}$$

9.
$$\begin{array}{r} 600 \\ \times\ 90 \\ \hline \end{array}$$

10.
$$\begin{array}{r} 4,400 \\ \times\ \ \ 30 \\ \hline \end{array}$$

11.
$$\begin{array}{r} 7,000 \\ \times\ \ \ 60 \\ \hline \end{array}$$

Use the table of contents to answer the questions.

12. On what page would you find fast-food restaurants? _____

13. On what page could you find out what the weather is like? _____

14. On what page would you look for movie listings? _____

15. On what page would you look for job openings? _____

16. On what page would you find bus schedules? _____

Coraville Happenings Guide
Local Information, Table of Contents

DAY 7

An *idiom* is an expression that means something other than what the individual words literally say. Underline the idiom in each sentence. Then, write what the idiom means.

17.   She was really pulling my leg.

_____

18.   Do you think we'll be in hot water?

_____

19.   Time flies when you are having fun.

_____

20.   You've hit the nail on the head, Shanice!

_____

21.   Ryan said that he will lend a hand tomorrow.

_____

Multiply to find each product.

| 22. | 39 × 69 | 23. | 72 × 18 | 24. | 85 × 36 | 25. | 23 × 87 | 26. | 46 × 77 |

| 27. | 57 × 49 | 28. | 41 × 73 | 29. | 48 × 95 | 30. | 88 × 66 | 31. | 68 × 92 |

FITNESS FLASH: Do five push-ups.

* See page ii.

PLACE STICKER HERE

Read each clue and write the mystery word.

- It is composed of mineral particles that are mixed with animal and plant matter.

- It is a well-organized, complicated layer of debris that covers most of the earth's land surface.

- It can be red or black, as well as many other shades and colors.

- It is one of the most important resources in any country.

- It takes a long time to form.

- Geologists say that it is the material that covers the rock below the earth's surface.

    Answer: _____

Solve each problem.

1. 5,162
    − 2,168

2. 9,252
    − 5,003

3. 7,825
    − 3,148

4. 3,529
    + 7,506

5. 8,929
    + 4,050

6. 9,341
    − 6,037

7. 2,629
    + 7,536

8. 4,528
    + 1,257

9. 7,932
    − 5,847

10. 9,826
    + 1,329

11. 4,723
    + 5,297

12. 3,872
    − 1,799

DAY 8

Divide to find each quotient.

13. 9 ÷ 3 = _____   90 ÷ 3 = _____   900 ÷ 3 = _____

14. 8 ÷ 2 = _____   80 ÷ 2 = _____   800 ÷ 2 = _____

15. 12 ÷ 4 = _____   120 ÷ 4 = _____   1,200 ÷ 4 = _____

16. 6 ÷ 3 = _____   60 ÷ 3 = _____   600 ÷ 3 = _____

17. 30 ÷ 6 = _____   300 ÷ 6 = _____   3,000 ÷ 6 = _____

18. 72 ÷ 8 = _____   720 ÷ 8 = _____   7,200 ÷ 8 = _____

19. 32 ÷ 8 = _____   320 ÷ 8 = _____   3,200 ÷ 8 = _____

20. 49 ÷ 7 = _____   490 ÷ 7 = _____   4,900 ÷ 7 = _____

On the line, write an antonym for each underlined word.

21. Does that fruit punch contain <u>artificial</u> coloring?   _____

22. The puppy was a bit <u>meek</u> during her first week in a new home.   _____

23. Turn the dial <u>counterclockwise</u> to wind the watch.   _____

24. Grandma and Grandpa were impressed by what a <u>graceful</u> dancer Sonya is.   _____

25. Is that a <u>rare</u> book?   _____

26. Mom wants to <u>encourage</u> Jamilla's interest in art.   _____

27. This a very <u>narrow</u> bridge!   _____

66

PLACE STICKER HERE

Divide to find each quotient.

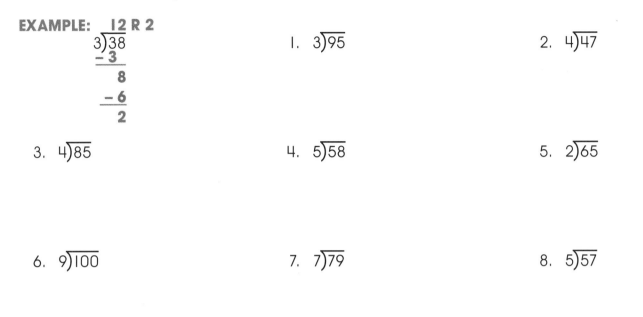

EXAMPLE:
```
   12 R 2
3)38
  -3
   8
  -6
   2
```

1. 3)95

2. 4)47

3. 4)85

4. 5)58

5. 2)65

6. 9)100

7. 7)79

8. 5)57

Write each word on the line. Draw a line between each syllable in the word. Use a dictionary to check your work.

EXAMPLE: column   _____col/umn_____

9. harness _____

10. liveliness _____

11. inflate _____

12. cable _____

13. glorious _____

14. washing _____

15. pigeon _____

16. apple _____

17. jewelry _____

18. maple _____

19. bicycle _____

20. frozen _____

21. difficult _____

22. tennis _____

23. happy _____

FACTOID: Millions of trees are accidentally planted by squirrels because they forget where they hid the nuts!

Look up the word *power* in a dictionary. Now, write a paragraph about someone or something that has power. Explain why you think this person or thing has power and how you think that came to be.

_____

_____

_____

_____

_____

_____

_____

_____

_____

_____

_____

_____

_____

FITNESS FLASH: Do 10 sit-ups.

* See page ii.

PLACE
STICKER
HERE

Subtract to find each difference. Write answers in simplest form.

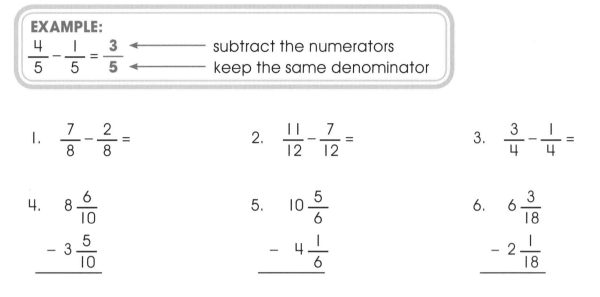

EXAMPLE:

$\dfrac{4}{5} - \dfrac{1}{5} = \dfrac{3}{5}$ ← subtract the numerators

← keep the same denominator

1. $\dfrac{7}{8} - \dfrac{2}{8} =$

2. $\dfrac{11}{12} - \dfrac{7}{12} =$

3. $\dfrac{3}{4} - \dfrac{1}{4} =$

4. $8\dfrac{6}{10}$
   $- 3\dfrac{5}{10}$
   _____

5. $10\dfrac{5}{6}$
   $- 4\dfrac{1}{6}$
   _____

6. $6\dfrac{3}{18}$
   $- 2\dfrac{1}{18}$
   _____

Write three ways to conserve each resource.

7. water _____

_____

8. trees _____

_____

9. oil _____

_____

10. wildlife habitats _____

_____

CHARACTER CHECK: Why is it important to be someone whom people can trust? How can you get and maintain a positive reputation? Write your answers on a separate sheet of paper.

DAY 10

Read the poem. Then, answer the questions.

from Rain in Summer
by Henry W. Longfellow

How beautiful is the rain!
After the dust and heat,
In the broad and fiery street,
In the narrow lane,
How beautiful is the rain!

How it clatters along the roofs,
Like the tramp of hoofs
How it gushes and struggles out
From the throat of the overflowing spout!

Across the window pane
It pours and pours;

And swift and wide,
With a muddy tide,
Like a river down the gutter roars
The rain, the welcome rain!

In the country, on every side,
Where far and wide,
Like a leopard's tawny and spotted hide,
Stretches the plain,
To the dry grass and the drier grain
How welcome is the rain!

11. Longfellow uses several similes in the poem. Choose one simile and write it on the line. Tell what two things are being compared.

_____

_____

12. Why is the author so joyful to have it rain?

_____

_____

13. How does the author's outlook affect the tone of the poem? Rewrite a line from the poem using a different tone.

_____

_____

PLACE
STICKER
HERE

When multiplying by powers of ten, count the number of zeros. Then, move the decimal point that many places to the right. Solve each problem by moving the decimal point.

EXAMPLE: 2.543×100 (Think: There are 2 zeros. Move the decimal point two places to the right.)

$2.543 \times 100 = 254.3$

1. $3.45 \times 10 =$ _____

2. $27.32 \times 100 =$ _____

3. $0.625 \times 1000 =$ _____

4. $254.35 \times 100 =$ _____

5. $0.017 \times 10 =$ _____

6. $0.98 \times 1000 =$ _____

7. $45.976 \times 10000 =$ _____

8. $18.526 \times 100 =$ _____

9. $100.53 \times 10 =$ _____

10. $78.287 \times 1000 =$ _____

The next time you watch TV or read a magazine, pay attention to the commercials or advertisements. In each box, write what you think is true and what you think is false about each commercial or advertisement you watched.

What is the commercial or advertisement about?	True	False
11.		
12.		
13.		

DAY II

Label each angle.

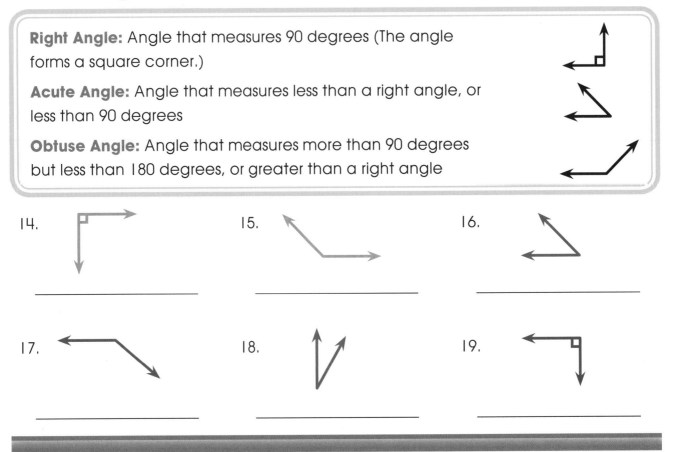

Right Angle: Angle that measures 90 degrees (The angle forms a square corner.)

Acute Angle: Angle that measures less than a right angle, or less than 90 degrees

Obtuse Angle: Angle that measures more than 90 degrees but less than 180 degrees, or greater than a right angle

14. _____

15. _____

16. _____

17. _____

18. _____

19. _____

The air contains water. Try this experiment to discover how water gets into the air.

- Get three or more drinking glasses that are all about the same size.

- Fill the glasses almost full of water.

- Place them in different areas, such as warm places, cool places, dark places, windy places, outside places, inside places, and other places of your choice.

- Watch them for four or five days. Check the water levels.

What happened to the water in the glasses? On a separate sheet of paper, explain in your own words where you think the water vapor in the atmosphere comes from and where it goes.

FACTOID: Adults blink about 10 times a minute, but babies blink only once or twice a minute.

PLACE STICKER HERE

Multiplication/Language Arts

Multiply to find each product.

1. 254
    × 12

2. 78
    × 14

3. 288
    × 22

4. 354
    × 15

5. 192
    × 34

6. 500
    × 14

7. 85
    × 74

8. 415
    × 31

9. 609
    × 24

Words in a series are separated by commas. Write the commas in each sentence.

10. Lin Paco Julie and Keesha are going to a movie.

11. Anna took her spelling reading and math books to school.

12. The snack bar is only open Monday Tuesday Friday and Saturday.

13. Our new school flag is blue green yellow black and orange.

14. Many women men children and pets enjoy sledding.

15. Have you seen the kittens chicks or goslings?

DAY 12

Read the passage. Then, answer the questions.

Bird Watching

Many people enjoy the hobby of bird watching. It is a pastime you can do in your own yard. If you put seeds in a bird feeder or hang a birdhouse, you are more likely to attract birds. You may notice that birds visit the feeder at certain times of day or that different birds prefer different types of foods. You may see baby birds trying their wings as they leave the nest for the first time. Some people travel to other parts of the world to see birds that they cannot see at home. They may use binoculars to get a better look at birds perching in trees or flying overhead. Some people keep lists of the species of birds they have seen. There are even contests to see who can spot the greatest variety of birds over a period of time!

16. What is the main idea of this passage?

    a.   Bird watching is a popular hobby that many people enjoy.

    b.   Some birds like to eat seeds, while others like fruit.

    c.   There are many different species of birds.

17. How can you attract more birds to your yard? _____

_____

18. What are some things you might notice about birds in your yard?

_____

_____

19. What do people use to help them see birds from a distance?_____

FITNESS FLASH: Do 10 lunges.

* See page ii.

PLACE
STICKER
HERE

The *perfect tense* is used to describe actions that have been completed. Underline the complete verb in perfect tense in each sentence.

1. Uncle Rico has taken Gabby to school each day this week.

2. The coach had noticed that the boys were tired at practice.

3. Audrey has been anxious to show you her new dance routine.

4. Brandon had read all the books in that series already.

5. By January, Moki will have earned enough money for a new bike.

6. The mail carrier had delivered the package at noon.

7. I will have thanked everyone who came to my party by the end of the week.

8. I have been calling the Carsons all day.

Find each quotient. Show your work.

9. 12)2,578

10. 32)6,457

11. 15)4,159

12. 22)1,548

13. 50)6,550

14. 14)1,848

15. 42)8,532

16. 35)4,565

17. 27)6,839

DAY 13

Underline the prepositional phrase in each sentence. On the line, write what question the prepositional phrase answers.

EXAMPLE: Ethan put his helmet <u>on the picnic table</u>. _____where_____

18. Jacob poured the lemon juice into the pitcher and stirred it. _____

19. The speckled tree frog hid beneath the glossy green leaf. _____

20. Nazim ran across the street to find the baseball. _____

21. Mr. Huang tried not to cough during the performance. _____

22. After the game, we're going straight home. _____

23. The yellow leaf landed in the stream. _____

24. Nora worked carefully and tried not to color outside the lines. _____

25. "I'd like to keep this information between you and me," confided Maddy. _____

Fact vs. Fiction

Honesty means telling the truth. Imagine that you and a friend are at the movies. Each of you orders a bag of popcorn, and the cashier accidentally gives you extra change. What do you do?

On another sheet of paper, draw two comic strips that start the same but end differently. The first comic should show the outcome of not being honest, and the second should show the outcome of being honest. Include at least four scenes in each comic strip to capture your thoughts.

FACTOID: The world's largest desert is the Sahara. It covers 3.5 million square miles (9 million km²) or about one-third of Africa.

Use a stopwatch or a watch with a second hand to time yourself as you do the following activities. Use that information to calculate how many times you could do them in 5 minutes, 8 minutes, 10 minutes, and 15 minutes. Fill in the chart.

1. How many times can you hop in one minute? _____

2. How many steps can you take in one minute? _____

3. How many jumping jacks can you do in one minute? _____

4. How many times can you toss a ball and catch it in one minute? _____

5. How many times can you bounce a ball in one minute? _____

Activity	Minutes				
	1	5	8	10	15
hop					
steps (walking)					
jumping jacks					
toss and catch ball					
bounce ball					

A comma belongs after the words *yes* and *no* when they begin a sentence. A comma also belongs before and/or after a person's name when the person is being addressed. Write commas where they belong in each sentence.

6. Yes I will go with you Tristan.

7. Wynona I am glad Zoe will come.

8. Aaron do you play tennis?

9. Yes I went to the doctor's office.

10. Raul do you want to go?

11. Neyla what happened?

12. No I never learned how to fish.

13. Mom thanks for the help.

14. No I need to finish this.

15. Hugo I found a penny.

16. Come on T.J. let's go to the game.

17. Tell me Crystal did you do this?

DAY 14

Write a story about your family. Tell who your family members are and what they are like.

_____

_____

_____

_____

_____

_____

_____

_____

_____

_____

_____

_____

Worth the "Weight"

Try adding a strength component to any physical activity. The next time you are ready to play or exercise, put on a backpack filled with soft, slightly weighted objects, such as small bags of sand. You will notice a small difference while you play or exercise. But, by the end of the summer, you will notice a big difference in your strength, especially if you gradually add more weight each time you exert yourself.

* See page ii.

Find the value of each expression. Do the operations inside parentheses ( ) first. Then, do the operations inside brackets [ ]. Finally, do the operations inside braces { }.

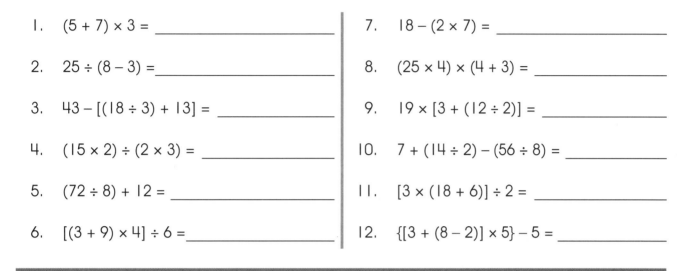

1. $(5 + 7) \times 3 =$ _____

2. $25 \div (8 - 3) =$ _____

3. $43 - [(18 \div 3) + 13] =$ _____

4. $(15 \times 2) \div (2 \times 3) =$ _____

5. $(72 \div 8) + 12 =$ _____

6. $[(3 + 9) \times 4] \div 6 =$ _____

7. $18 - (2 \times 7) =$ _____

8. $(25 \times 4) \times (4 + 3) =$ _____

9. $19 \times [3 + (12 \div 2)] =$ _____

10. $7 + (14 \div 2) - (56 \div 8) =$ _____

11. $[3 \times (18 + 6)] \div 2 =$ _____

12. $\{[3 + (8 - 2)] \times 5\} - 5 =$ _____

Write any missing periods, question marks, exclamation points, commas, quotation marks, or capitalization in each sentence.

13. Nate, do you have the map of our town asked Kit

14. What an exciting day I had cried Janelle

15. I said the puppy chewed up my sneaker

16. Did you know that birds' bones are hollow asked Mrs. Tyler

17. She answered no I did not know that

18. Wayne exclaimed I won first prize in the pie-baking contest

19. I'm tired after raking the yard said Sadie

20. I am too replied Sarah

FITNESS FLASH: Do 10 squats.

* See page ii.

DAY 15

Read the passage. Then, answer the questions.

Science Experiments

Scientists learn about the world by conducting experiments. They take careful notes about the instruments they use and the results they find. They share their discoveries with others so that everyone learns more about their subjects. You can do experiments, too! The library has many books with safe experiments that use balloons, water, or baking soda. You can learn how light travels or why marbles roll down a ramp. Ask an adult to help you choose and set up an experiment and to watch to make sure you are being safe. Be sure to clean up the area and wash your hands afterward. Take good notes about your work. By changing only one thing, the next time you do the experiment, you may get a completely different result. The important thing is not to worry if your results are not what you expected. Some of the greatest scientific discoveries in the world were made by accident!

21. What is the main idea of this passage?

  a. Children can do experiments as long as they are safe.

  b. Scientists often make mistakes that lead to great discoveries.

  c. You should always take good notes when conducting an experiment.

22. What kinds of information do scientists write in their notes? _____

_____

23. What happens when scientists share their findings with others? _____

_____

24. Why should you ask an adult to help? _____

_____

CHARACTER CHECK: At the beginning of one day, tell a family member three good things that are going to happen to you that day.

Write the month or the name of each U.S. holiday or special day. Use a calendar if you need help.

1. Be sure to wear green on March 17. It's_____ .

2. Send your sweetheart a card on February 14. It's_____ .

3. On July 4, the United States celebrates _____ .

4. October 31 can be really scary. It's _____ .

5. Do you work on _____ in September?

6. Martin Luther King, Jr.'s birthday is in _____ .

7. Americans celebrate this parent's day in June. _____

Circle the word that is on the dictionary page with each pair of guide words.

8. bowling • brain

   bread   braid   brave

9. liquid • litter

   list   live   lion

10. monster • more

    money   monsoon   moon

11. work • worst

    word   world   worth

12. gold • gossamer

    gondola   goal   gourd

13. spoon • spread

    spoil   spring   spray

14. flank • flaw

    flash   flame   flight

15. central • chafe

    cell   chalet   certain

DAY 16

Circle the two words in each group that are spelled correctly.

16.
gabel
genuine
gracefull
graine
great

17.
suger
surpize
terrible
straight
sonday

18.
allready
among
aunte
awhile
addvise

19.
where
weather
wite
weare
rotee

20.
jackit
junior
jujment
justece
journey

21.
rimind
remain
fouff
refer
raisd

22.
feathers
feever
finsih
folow
fiction

23.
donkiys
doubble
drawer
dosen
detective

24.
handsum
herrd
holiday
healthy
haevy

25.
explore
elctrecity
enjine
enormous
ecstat

Underline the conjunction (or conjunction pair) in each sentence below.

26. I thought the story was short but exciting.

27. Both Logan and Antoine are taking rock climbing lessons.

28. After you take a bath, brush your teeth.

29. Neither the library nor the bookstore is open on Sunday.

30. Isla baked muffins on Saturday morning and made crepes on Sunday morning.

31. Since Kazuo's birthday is on Monday, we're celebrating this weekend.

FACTOID: Hummingbirds are the only birds that can hover and fly upside down.

PLACE
STICKER
HERE

Write each missing numerator.

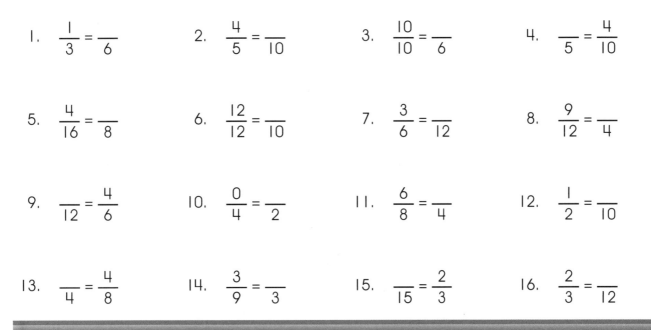

1. $\dfrac{1}{3} = \dfrac{}{6}$

2. $\dfrac{4}{5} = \dfrac{}{10}$

3. $\dfrac{10}{10} = \dfrac{}{6}$

4. $\dfrac{}{5} = \dfrac{4}{10}$

5. $\dfrac{4}{16} = \dfrac{}{8}$

6. $\dfrac{12}{12} = \dfrac{}{10}$

7. $\dfrac{3}{6} = \dfrac{}{12}$

8. $\dfrac{9}{12} = \dfrac{}{4}$

9. $\dfrac{}{12} = \dfrac{4}{6}$

10. $\dfrac{0}{4} = \dfrac{}{2}$

11. $\dfrac{6}{8} = \dfrac{}{4}$

12. $\dfrac{1}{2} = \dfrac{}{10}$

13. $\dfrac{}{4} = \dfrac{4}{8}$

14. $\dfrac{3}{9} = \dfrac{}{3}$

15. $\dfrac{}{15} = \dfrac{2}{3}$

16. $\dfrac{2}{3} = \dfrac{}{12}$

Write the correct word for each definition.

schedule	campaign	artificial	reputation
assistant	exchange	publicize	genuine

17.   not natural, not real _____

18.   a timed plan for a project _____

19.   a giving or taking of one thing for another _____

20.   an opinion in which a person is commonly held _____

21.   a person who serves or helps _____

22.   being what it is said to be; true or real _____

23.   a series of planned actions, often to get someone elected _____

24.   to make information known _____

DAY 17

Read the letter. Then, answer the questions.

September 24, 1849

Dear Thomas,

I'm finally settled in and have a chance to write. The trip west was rough and not quite something you can prepare for. You wouldn't believe the sickness I saw, even in strong, healthy folks. Water was scarce, but I was real careful about my supply. Picturing piles of gold in California kept me moving.

I think you know why I'm writing, Thomas. I want you to pack up and join me here in California. You'll make more money than you ever thought possible. Then you can go home, pay off the mortgage on the farm, and marry Elizabeth.

The riverbeds are filled with gold, Thomas—just waiting for you to come and pan it. You don't want to miss this opportunity for I know you'd regret it. You write back and let me know what you decide. Give my love to the family. And tell all of them not to worry about me. I'll strike it rich and come home and take care of everybody in style.

Your devoted brother,
Albert

25. Write a short summary of the letter.

_____

_____

26. How would this text be different if it were not told from a first-person point of view? _____

_____

27. What can you infer about how the narrator feels about his decision to go west?

_____

FITNESS FLASH: Do five push-ups.

* See page ii.

PLACE
STICKER
HERE

Read each sentence. Add quotation marks around titles where they are needed. Underline titles that would be italicized in type.

1. I read Charlie and the Chocolate Factory during summer vacation.

2. Jorge and Will are planning to rent The Lego Movie.

3. Samantha memorized three poems from the book Where the Sidewalk Ends.

4. On the last day of camp, we sang the Woody Guthrie song This Land Is Your Land for all the parents.

5. The high school drama club is doing a production of the play Romeo and Juliet.

6. Aunt Anya's favorite poem is Afternoon on a Hill by Edna St. Vincent Millay.

7. Danita knows all the words to the song Let It Go from the movie Frozen.

8. Every December, my family watches the movie Miracle on 34th Street.

For each number, write the digit in the given place.

thousands	hundreds	tens	ones	tenths	hundredths	thousandths
1	3	2	4 .	9	7	3

9. 46,251.25

   thousands _____

10. 524.326

    hundredths _____

11. 255,024.01

    tens _____

12. 25.314

    tenths _____

13. 254,326,845

    ones _____

14. 245,326.487

    thousandths _____

DAY 18

A *simile* is a figure of speech that compares two things using the words *as* or *like*. Complete each simile.

EXAMPLE: The bedsheets were as **white as a snowy owl.**

15. Her eyes were like _____

16. The night was as dark as _____

17. His legs were as _____

It is a good idea to have a first-aid kit in your home. A first-aid kit contains supplies, such as bandages and ointments, that would help you in an emergency. Make a list of the things you would put in your first-aid kit and explain why.

_____

_____

_____

_____

_____

_____

_____

_____

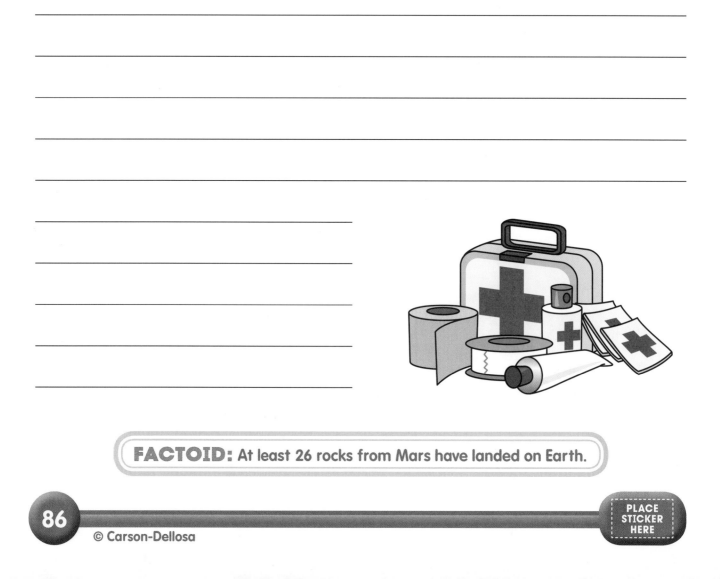

FACTOID: At least 26 rocks from Mars have landed on Earth.

PLACE STICKER HERE

Write a sentence for each interjection from the word bank. Remember, interjections are often followed by an exclamation point.

EXAMPLE: Aw! I'm so sorry you'll have to miss the party!

oops	wow	hurray	goodness	ouch	hey

1. _____

2. _____

3. _____

4. _____

5. _____

6. _____

Rewrite each decimal in number form on the line. Then, order the decimals from least to greatest value.

7. one and thirty-six hundredths _____

8. four and twenty-three thousandths _____

9. five tenths _____

10. forty-seven hundredths _____

11. eight hundred thirty-three thousandths _____

12. twelve hundredths _____

_____ _____ _____ _____ _____ _____

DAY 19

A *survey* is a series of questions about a product or an issue. Conduct a survey of your neighbors, friends, or relatives on how many pets they have and what kind. Think of questions you can ask. Use the space below to take notes. Then, record the results in a report, chart, graph, table, or picture.

_____

_____

_____

_____

_____

_____

Multiply. Write answers in simplest form.

13. $\dfrac{1}{2} \times \dfrac{3}{4} =$ _____

14. $5 \times \dfrac{2}{5} =$ _____

15. $\dfrac{3}{7} \times \dfrac{5}{8} =$ _____

16. $3 \times \dfrac{11}{12} =$ _____

17. $\dfrac{4}{9} \times \dfrac{1}{2} =$ _____

18. $\dfrac{12}{15} \times \dfrac{3}{5} =$ _____

19. $\dfrac{2}{3} \times \dfrac{5}{6} =$ _____

20. $\dfrac{1}{4} \times 9 =$ _____

21. $\dfrac{4}{7} \times \dfrac{2}{7} =$ _____

22. $6 \times \dfrac{4}{5} =$ _____

23. $\dfrac{1}{2} \times \dfrac{2}{9} =$ _____

24. $\dfrac{7}{8} \times 8 =$ _____

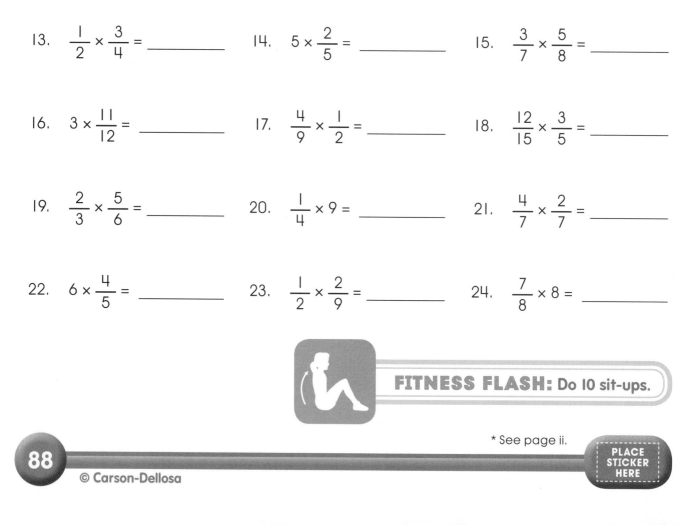

FITNESS FLASH: Do 10 sit-ups.

* See page ii.

PLACE STICKER HERE

There is an incorrect shift in verb tense in each sentence. Cross out the incorrect verb and write the verb in the correct tense on the line.

1. The actor glanced down at the script and then recites his lines.

   _____

2. My family goes to the same restaurant each year for Dad's birthday and we loved it.

   _____

3. Tomorrow, Ms. Handel will go to the art museum, and she met her sister for lunch.

   _____

4. Sophia gathered some kindling, and Myles will dry the dishes.

   _____

5. Next year, Manuel will be in the Sparkling Starfish swim class, and Lea is in the Blazing Barnacles class.

   _____

6. Teresa's house has a large oak tree in the front yard, and it was across the street from the school.

   _____

Solve each problem. Write answers in simplest form.

7. A farmer divided her field into four sections and planted one crop per section. What fraction of the field is planted with wheat?

   _____ of the field

8. Each floor of a parking garage can hold 90 cars. When all the floors of the garage are full, there are 450 cars in the garage altogether. What fraction of the cars is parked on the ground floor?

   _____ of the cars

9. A pizza is cut into 12 slices. If 3 friends share the pizza equally, what fraction of the pizza does each friend eat?

   _____ of the pizza

10. Louis bought a box of 85 marbles. He gave 17 marbles each to 5 friends. What fraction of the marbles did he give to each friend?

    _____ of the marbles

DAY 20

Complete each sentence by circling the word that is spelled correctly.

11. The big cat couldn't _____ the tree.

    a. climb   b. climbe   c. climmb   d. clibm

12. We paid $100 for _____ .

    a. groseries   b. groceeries   c. groceries   d. grosserys

13. Chad is a very _____ person.

    a. kreative   b. creative   c. createive   d. crative

14. We love to _____ ride in the winter.

    a. sleigh   b. sleia   c. cleigh   d. slagh

15. I found the perfect _____ for my science project.

    a. matterial   b. maririal   c. metariel   d. material

Make a list of things that use electricity. Then, write about what you think life would be like without electricity.

_____

_____

_____

_____

CHARACTER CHECK: What does it mean to be a good friend? On a separate sheet of paper, make a list of 10 traits that a good friend should have. Why are these traits important for a strong friendship?

PLACE STICKER HERE

Trust Metal to Rust

Will iron nails placed in water rust faster and lose more mass than iron nails placed in sand?

Materials:
- 2 identical glass jars
- 10 iron nails
- 200 mL (6.75 ounces) of distilled water
- balance
- paper towels
- 200 mL (6.75 ounces) of very dry sand

Procedure:

1. Put 200 mL of sand into one jar and 200 mL of water into the other jar.

2. Use the balance to find the mass of five nails. Record the mass in the table. Place the nails in the sand in the first jar.

3. Use the balance to find the mass of the remaining five nails. Record the mass in the table. Place the second group of nails in the water in the second jar. Leave both jars in a safe place overnight.

4. The next day, remove the nails from the jar of sand. Place them on a clean, dry paper towel. Remove excess sand but do not rub the nails.

5. Place the nails on the balance. Record their mass on the data table. Then, place the nails back into the jar of sand. Repeat with the nails in the jar of water.

6. Continue to collect data for three more days. Record your results in the table.

Day	Nails in Sand		Nails in Water	
	Mass	Observations	Mass	Observations
1				
2				
3				
4				
5				

BONUS

Screening the Sun

There are many different brands of sunscreen with various SPF ratings. The SPF, or sun protection factor, tells you how long the sunscreen will protect your skin. To find out if higher SPF sunscreens really provide better protection, try the following experiment.

Materials:
- 4 ultraviolet (UV) detection beads (available from scientific supply companies)
- 3 bottles of sunscreen (the same brand with different SPFs)
- tray (lined with paper)
- stopwatch

Procedure:
1. Obtain four UV beads of the same color. These beads are coated with a special chemical that makes them change color when exposed to UV light. The darker the color, the stronger the UV light.

2. Rub a small amount of one sunscreen over a bead and place it on the lined tray. Label the bead with the sunscreen's SPF. Repeat with two more beads and the other sunscreens. Make sure that you use the same amount of sunscreen on each bead.

3. Place the fourth bead on the tray with no sunscreen as a control, or comparison, bead. Label this bead *control*.

4. Set the tray in the sun. Rate the beads according to color after one minute. A rating of one means the bead stayed completely white, while a rating of five is the darkest color possible (the control bead).

5. Leave the beads in the sun for one hour and rate them again. Record the data in a table.

Write a letter or an e-mail to a friend or relative. Tell about the experiment you did. Explain how it works and what your results were.

* See page ii.

New Zealand

Use the map of New Zealand to answer the questions.

1. On which island is the city of Christchurch located?

   a. South Island

   b. North Island

   c. Stewart Island

2. Gisborne is _____ of Dunedin.

   a. northeast

   b. northwest

   c. southeast

3. The capital of New Zealand is _____.

   a. Auckland

   b. Wellington

   c. New Plymouth

4. The distance between Greymouth and Christchurch is approximately _____.

   a. 150 kilometers

   b. 75 kilometers

   c. 300 kilometers

N
W E
S

Dargaville •

Auckland •

NORTH
ISLAND   Gisborne •

New Plymouth •

• Napier

T a s m a n

S e a

Palmerston •
North

*Tasman
Bay*

★ **Wellington**

*Cook
Strait*

Westport •

Greymouth •

NEW ZEALAND

Pegasus Bay

• Christchurch

P a c i f i c

O c e a n

SOUTH
ISLAND

• Dunedin

Invercargill •

STEWART
ISLAND

New Zealand

★ National Capital

• Major Cities

0   150 Miles

0   150 KM

BONUS

Australia

Use the map of Australia to answer the questions.

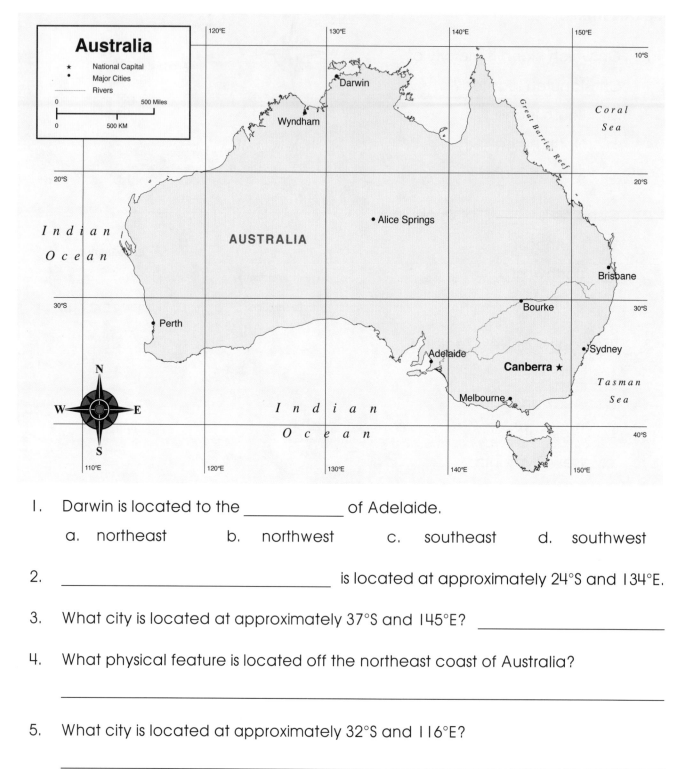

1. Darwin is located to the _____ of Adelaide.

    a. northeast   b. northwest   c. southeast   d. southwest

2. _____ is located at approximately 24°S and 134°E.

3. What city is located at approximately 37°S and 145°E? _____

4. What physical feature is located off the northeast coast of Australia?

    _____

5. What city is located at approximately 32°S and 116°E?

    _____

Countries of Oceania

Use the maps below to answer the questions.

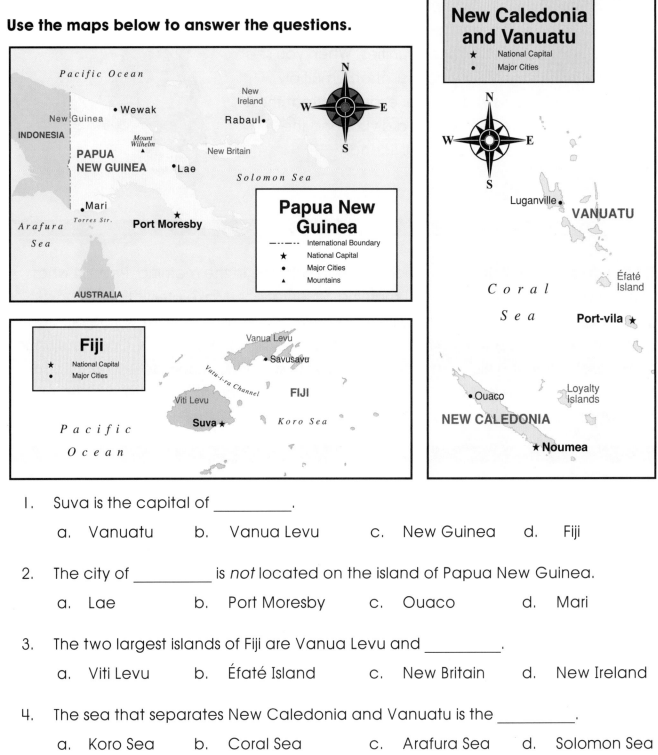

1. Suva is the capital of _____.

   a. Vanuatu   b. Vanua Levu   c. New Guinea   d. Fiji

2. The city of _____ is *not* located on the island of Papua New Guinea.

   a. Lae   b. Port Moresby   c. Ouaco   d. Mari

3. The two largest islands of Fiji are Vanua Levu and _____.

   a. Viti Levu   b. Éfaté Island   c. New Britain   d. New Ireland

4. The sea that separates New Caledonia and Vanuatu is the _____.

   a. Koro Sea   b. Coral Sea   c. Arafura Sea   d. Solomon Sea

BONUS

Take It Outside!

Keep your math skills sharp this summer by taking advantage of calculation opportunities. When you see a number grouping, quickly add, subtract, multiply, or divide the numbers you see. For example, treat the first number on a license plate as a divisor and the remaining three numbers as the dividend.

Take a pen or pencil and a notebook outside with you in the morning. Record what you see and hear. Reflect on your morning observations. Make predictions of how things will look and sound at nighttime. What will be the same? What will be different? That night, go outside with an adult and record the sights and sounds. Compare your notes about day and night activity. How did your predictions compare to what you saw and heard at night? What might have caused your predictions to be different than what you observed?

Many animals rely on their sense of hearing to explore their environments. You can do the same thing on a summer afternoon. With an adult, sit in your backyard, on a park bench, or in some other safe and comfortable place. Open a notebook to a blank sheet of paper. With a pen or pencil, draw a star in the middle of the paper to represent yourself. Then, close your eyes and listen to the world around you. With your eyes closed, make small marks on the paper to describe the sounds you hear and the directions they are coming from. For example, you could draw a wavy line to represent the gurgling of a small stream or a swirl to represent the rush of wind through the trees. After a few minutes, open your eyes and examine your paper. How much could you tell about your surroundings just by listening?

* See page ii.

Monthly Goals

Think of three goals to set for yourself this month. For example, you may want to read for 30 minutes each day. Write your goals on the lines and review them with an adult.

Place a sticker next to each goal that you complete. Feel proud that you have met your goals!

1. _____ PLACE STICKER HERE

2. _____ PLACE STICKER HERE

3. _____ PLACE STICKER HERE

Word List

The following words are used in this section. They are good words for you to know. Read each word aloud. Use a dictionary to look up each word that you do not know. Then, write two sentences. Use a word from the word list in each sentence.

chart   mental
climate   symbols
economy   system
legend   temperature

1. _____

_____

2. _____

_____

Introduction to Endurance

Physical Endurance

What do playing tag, jumping rope, and riding your bike have in common? They are all great ways to build endurance!

Having endurance means doing an activity for a long time before your body becomes tired. Your heart is stronger when you have endurance. Your muscles receive more oxygen.

Use the warm summer mornings and sunny days to go outside. Pick activities that you enjoy. Invite a family member on a walk or a bike ride. Play a game of basketball with friends. Leave the less active times for when it is dark, too hot, or raining.

Set an endurance goal this summer. For example, you might jump rope every day until you can jump for two minutes without stopping. Set new goals when you meet your old ones. Be proud of your endurance success!

Endurance and Character Development

Showing mental endurance means sticking with something. You can show mental endurance every day. Staying with a task when you might want to quit and keeping at it until it is done are ways that you can show mental endurance.

Build your mental endurance this summer. Think of a time when you were frustrated or bored. Maybe you wanted to take swimming lessons. But, after a few early morning lessons, it is not as fun as you imagined. Think about some key points, such as how you asked all spring to take lessons. Be positive. Remind yourself that you have taken only a few lessons. You might get used to the early morning lessons. Think of ways to make the lessons more enjoyable, such as sleeping a few extra minutes during the morning car ride. Quitting should be the last option.

Build your mental endurance now. It will help prepare you for challenges you may face later!

Fill the blanks in each sentence with a set of correlative conjunctions from the word bank.

| either/or | neither/nor | both/and | not only/but also |

1. _____ my uncle _____ my aunt will be able to attend Claudia's graduation.

2. _____ we can go to the basketball game, _____ we can go to the water park.

3. We often see_____ cardinals _____ chickadees at the feeder in our backyard.

4. _____did Marco forget his math homework today, _____ he _____ lost a library book.

5. _____ our cats _____ our dog behave very well when we go on vacation.

6. _____ the maple _____ the chestnut tree have grown a lot in the last couple of years.

Three Times the Fitness

A *triathlon* is an intense endurance race with swimming, cycling, and running events. This kind of athletic event requires incredible strength, flexibility, and endurance. Set up your own mini-triathlon to test your endurance. With an adult's help, plan a day where you can swim, bike, and run. For a variation, choose any three physical activities you prefer.

Try this activity several times throughout the summer. Start with short distances. Gradually increase the distance to build your stamina. Track your distance over the summer. How much farther were you able to travel by the end of August?

* See page ii.

DAY 1

Read the passage. Then, answer the questions.

Latitude and Longitude

Latitude and longitude lines divide the earth into regions. Latitude lines run around the globe from east to west. The line around the middle is called the *equator*. Latitude is measured using the equator as zero. The lines around the earth as you move north are either labeled with positive numbers or the letter *N* for north. The lines going south have either negative numbers or the letter *S* for south. Longitude lines run north to south from the north pole to the south pole. The zero point, or the *Prime Meridian*, for longitude runs through Greenwich, England. The numbers east of the Prime Meridian are either labeled with positive numbers or the letter *E* for east. The numbers west of the Prime Meridian are either labeled with negative numbers or the letter *W* for west. Both measurements are given in degrees. The latitude of Ottawa, the capital of Canada, is 45°25'0" N, which is read as "forty-five degrees, twenty-five minutes, zero seconds north." Latitude and longitude have long been used by people who study geography and mapmaking, as well as by explorers who travel around the world.

7. What is the main idea of this passage?

    a. Latitude and longitude lines are used to divide the earth into regions.

    b. Longitude is measured in degrees.

    c. The latitude of Ottawa is 45°25'0" N.

8. Where is the zero point for longitude? _____

9. Which people might use latitude and longitude most often? _____

    _____

10. Why do you think people might want to know their exact locations on the earth?

    _____

    _____

PLACE
STICKER
HERE

Circle the electric circuit words in the puzzle. Words can go across and down.

current	closed circuit	negative	watts
metal	battery	positive	wires
insulator	conductor	voltage	resistance

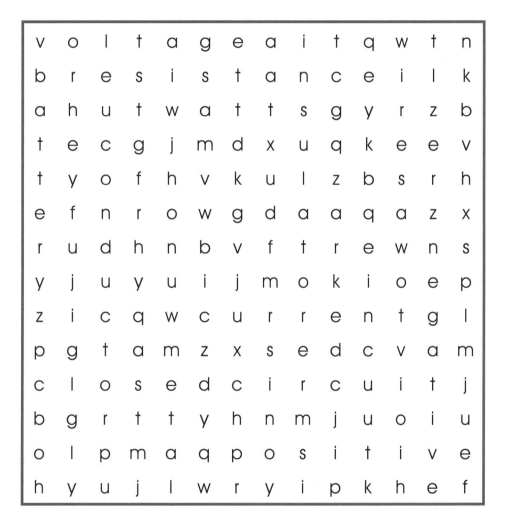

```
v o l t a g e a i t q w t n
b r e s i s t a n c e i l k
a h u t w a t t s g y r z b
t e c g j m d x u q k e e v
t y o f h v k u l z b s r h
e f n r o w g d a a q a z x
r u d h n b v f t r e w n s
y j u y u i j m o k i o e p
z i c q w c u r r e n t g l
p g t a m z x s e d c v a m
c l o s e d c i r c u i t j
b g r t t y h n m j u o i u
o l p m a q p o s i t i v e
h y u j l w r y i p k h e f
```

DAY 2

Solve each division problem. To divide fractions, multiply the first fraction by the *reciprocal*, or reversed version, of the second fraction. It will help to change whole numbers into fractions.

EXAMPLE: $6 \div \dfrac{1}{6} = \dfrac{6}{1} \times \dfrac{6}{1} = \dfrac{36}{1} = 36$

1. $5 \div \dfrac{1}{2} = $ _____

2. $\dfrac{1}{5} \div 8 = $ _____

3. $\dfrac{1}{4} \div 7 = $ _____

4. $3 \div \dfrac{1}{3} = $ _____

5. $2 \div \dfrac{1}{9} = $ _____

6. $\dfrac{1}{8} \div 3 = $ _____

7. $9 \div \dfrac{1}{5} = $ _____

8. $\dfrac{1}{6} \div 5 = $ _____

9. $\dfrac{1}{3} \div 4 = $ _____

10. $4 \div \dfrac{1}{4} = $ _____

11. $7 \div \dfrac{1}{2} = $ _____

12. $\dfrac{1}{9} \div 3 = $ _____

Use editing marks to correct the punctuation and capitalization in the letter.

july 17 2015

dear david

thank you for sending me the pictures from your trip it looks like you had a great time do you want me to send them back

next week im going to kansas city with my dad i can't wait

your friend

greg

FITNESS FLASH: Jog in place for 30 seconds.

* See page ii.

Write an expression for each phrase and give its value.

EXAMPLE: 4 more than the product of 6 and 3   (6 × 3) + 4 = 18 + 4 = 22

1.   the difference of 15 and 7 divided by 2   _____

2.   the quotient of 56 and 8 multiplied by 4   _____

3.   12 less than the product of 5 and 9   _____

4. $\frac{1}{2}$ of 12 multiplied by the sum of 3 and 2   _____

5.   the difference of 8 and 1 multiplied by the product of 3 and 3   _____

6.   10 more than the quotient of 24 and 8   _____

Write a letter to a friend, a grandparent, or someone else of your choice. Make sure your letter contains all five parts of a letter: date, greeting, body, closing, and signature.

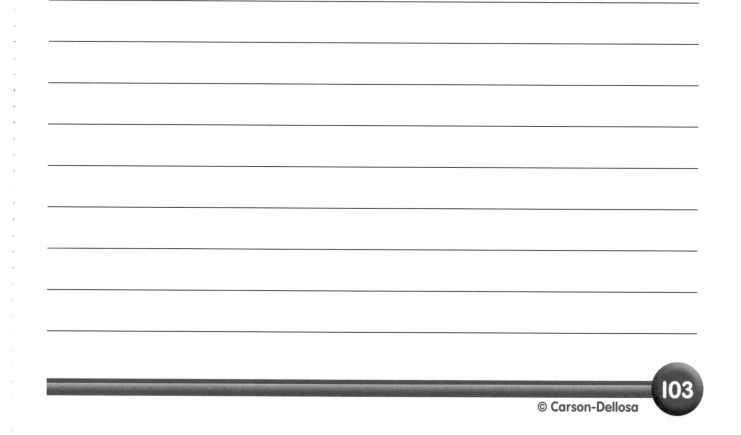

DAY 3

Read the passage. Then, answer the questions.

Political Parties

Political parties are groups of people who feel the same way about one or more issues. Each party may work to elect several candidates to office, from city mayor to the president of the United States. Political parties often use symbols to represent themselves. When people see the symbols, they think of the political parties. The donkey was first used in a political advertisement to represent President Andrew Jackson, who was with the U.S. Democratic Party. Donkeys are considered smart and courageous. The U.S. Republican Party symbol is the elephant. Elephants are known for their strength and intelligence. Both of these parties use red, white, and blue—the colors of the U.S. flag. Many of the Canadian political parties have maple leaves as part of their logos or designs to indicate that the parties are tied to their country. The maple leaf appears on the Canadian flag. Political parties in Great Britain use different symbols. The Labour Party uses the rose (the national flower), the Conservative Party uses the oak tree (for strength), and the Liberal Democrats use a dove (for peace).

7. What is the main idea of this passage?

    a. When people see a symbol, they think of a political party.

    b. Political parties use symbols to represent them.

    c. The Canadian flag has a maple leaf on it.

8. What are political parties? _____

    _____

9. Why do you think a political party might use symbols from its country's flag?

    _____

    _____

10. What symbols are used by British political parties? _____

FACTOID: A group of frogs is called an *army.*

104

PLACE STICKER HERE

Use the information below to convert each measurement.

| 16 ounces = 1 pound | 2,000 pounds = 1 ton |

1. 160 ounces = _____ pounds   2. _____ ounces = 5 pounds

3. 5 tons = _____ pounds   4. _____ ounces = 9 pounds

5. 4,000 pounds = _____ tons   6. _____ pounds = 7 tons

7. 8,000 pounds = _____ tons   8. _____ ounces = 11 pounds

9. _____ pounds = 3 tons   10. 10 tons = _____ pounds

11. 32 ounces = _____ pounds   12. _____ ounces = 3 pounds

Change one or both fractions in each problem so that both fractions have a common denominator. Then, add or subtract. Write the answer in simplest form.

13. $\frac{3}{4} + \frac{5}{8} =$ _____   14. $\frac{2}{9} + \frac{5}{6} =$ _____   15. $\frac{13}{15} - \frac{1}{3} =$ _____

16. $1\frac{1}{2} + \frac{5}{6} =$ _____   17. $2\frac{2}{3} - \frac{7}{12} =$ _____   18. $\frac{5}{13} + \frac{1}{3} =$ _____

19. $\frac{11}{12} - \frac{8}{15} =$ _____   20. $5\frac{1}{4} - 3\frac{5}{8} =$ _____   21. $\frac{9}{10} - \frac{3}{7} =$ _____

DAY 4

Write the correct word(s) to complete each sentence.

water	calcium	circulatory	cells	iron	digestive

22. The human body is made up of millions of tiny _____ .

23. The human body is mostly _____ , between 55 and 75 percent.

24. The human body has many metals and minerals in it, two of which are

    _____ and _____ .

25. The salivary glands, esophagus, stomach, gallbladder, large intestines, and

    small intestines are part of the _____ system.

26. The _____ system moves blood throughout the body.

Using a thesaurus, write one synonym and one antonym for each word.

	Synonym	Antonym
27. rough	_____	_____
28. problem	_____	_____
29. interesting	_____	_____
30. surprise	_____	_____
31. happy	_____	_____
32. harvest	_____	_____

FITNESS FLASH: Hop on your right foot for 30 seconds.

* See page ii.

PLACE STICKER HERE

Use the chart to answer each question.

Popular Joke Web Sites

Web Site	Number of Visitors
ruhilarious.joke	83,121
lapsincomedy.joke	58,452
webofpuns.joke	70,907
quietquippers.joke	46,162
dropmeapunchline.joke	49,323

1. Which Web site was the least popular? _____

2. Which Web site was the most popular? _____

3. How many more visitors did the most popular site receive than the least

    popular site? _____

4. How many more visitors did *webofpuns.joke* receive than *lapsincomedy.joke*?

    _____

5. How many fewer visitors did *dropmeapunchline.joke* receive than

    lapsincomedy.joke? _____

6. What is the average number of people who visited these Web sites? To find the

    average, divide the total number of visitors by the number of Web sites.

    _____

DAY 5

Read the passage. Then, answer the questions.

Reading Maps

Have you ever used a map to plan a route? A world map shows the outlines of the continents and seas. It may have parts shaded brown and green to show areas of desert or forest. A city map shows important buildings, such as the library or city hall, as well as city streets. Maps use symbols to help you understand them. A compass rose looks like an eight-pointed star inside a circle. It shows you the directions north, south, east, and west. North is usually at the top. A map scale tells you how the distances on a map relate to the real world. For example, one inch (2.5 cm) on the map may be equal to 100 miles (160.9 km). A map legend shows you what other symbols mean. A black dot may stand for a city, a star inside a circle may mean a country's capital city, and an airplane may be used to represent an airport. Knowing what these symbols mean makes it much easier to travel.

7. What is the main idea of this passage?

   a. Some maps use a compass rose and a scale.

   b. A world map is very different from a city map.

   c. Maps use symbols to help you understand them.

8. What does a world map show? _____

   _____

9. What does a city map show? _____

   _____

10. What does a compass rose show? _____

   _____

CHARACTER CHECK: What is the golden rule? On a separate sheet of paper, explain the rule using your own words.

PLACE STICKER HERE

Use the place value chart to write each number.

Hundred Millions	Ten Millions	Millions	Hundred Thousands	Ten Thousands	Thousands	Hundreds	Tens	Ones
	8	6	5	3	7	1	4	3

EXAMPLE: Eighty-six million five hundred thirty-seven thousand one hundred forty-three

86,537,143

1. Six million eight hundred forty-three thousand _____

2. Nine hundred six million four hundred thousand two _____

3. 986,218,320 _____

4. 234,186,018 _____

Write a self-portrait poem.

Write your name.
Write two words that describe you.
Write three words that tell what you like to do.
Write two more words that describe you.
Write your name again.

DAY 6

Read the passage. Then, answer the questions.

Paul Bunyan

Paul Bunyan was born in the woods of Maine. As soon as his parents saw their little giant, Pa headed straight for the nearest army post to ask for some old tents. He used them as diapers for his big boy!

The family kept an entire herd of dairy cows just to fill Paul's belly with milk when he was a young 'un. When Paul started crawling, he'd knock over trees without meaning to. The trouble didn't stop there. On a trip to the coast, Paul flooded a number of small towns just by splashing about in the ocean. The good folks of Maine had had enough. They asked Paul's parents to take their jumbo son and move somewhere he could have a bit more space.

The Bunyans settled in Minnesota. That year, Paul made his first friend—a gigantic, baby blue ox named Babe. Paul and Babe left giant footprints behind from frolicking around on a spring day. The rains came and filled up the holes, creating lakes. Paul and Babe were the reason that Minnesota became known as *the land of ten thousand lakes*.

5. Exaggeration is often used in legends and tall tales. Give examples of parts of Paul Bunyan's story that are exaggerated.

    _____

    _____

6. What is the author's purpose in writing this selection? How do you know?

    _____

    _____

7. The story of Paul Bunyan is a tall tale with many different retellings. Find another version online or at the library. How is it similar to and different from this version? Write a paragraph on a separate sheet of paper to explain, making sure to support your comparison with good details.

Use equivalent fractions to solve each problem. Write answers in simplest form.

1. Lacey practiced the piano three times yesterday. She practiced $\frac{1}{2}$ hour in the morning, $1\frac{1}{4}$ hours after school, and $\frac{3}{8}$ hour before bed. How long did she practice altogether?

    _____ hours

2. Max's pumpkin weighs $4\frac{4}{5}$ pounds. Lance's pumpkin weighs $6\frac{1}{3}$ pound. How much heavier is Lance's pumpkin than Max's?

    _____ pounds

3. The recipe calls for 3 cups of flour, $\frac{1}{2}$ cup of sugar, and $\frac{2}{3}$ cup of milk. What is the total volume of the three ingredients?

    _____ cups

4. The Mountain Spring Trail is $4\frac{7}{8}$ miles long. Hallee and Sophia have hiked $2\frac{11}{12}$ miles of the trail. How much farther do they have left to go?

    _____ miles

One word in each set is spelled incorrectly. Underline the misspelled word and write the correct spelling on the line. You may use a dictionary if needed.

5. eagle   melody   teknique   _____

6. express   migrasion   increase   _____

7. Febuary   autumn   receive   _____

8. admitted   impashent   politician   _____

9. scisors   visual   committee   _____

10. vessel   commotion   seperate   _____

FACTOID: Dragonflies can fly at speeds of up to 40 miles (64 km) per hour.

DAY 7

An *analogy* is a comparison between two word pairs. Complete each analogy.

EXAMPLE: Story is to <u>read</u> as song is to _____ <u>sing</u> _____ .

11.   <u>Brother</u> is to <u>boy</u> as <u>sister</u> is to _____ .

12.   <u>Princess</u> is to <u>queen</u> as <u>prince</u> is to _____ .

13.   <u>Milk</u> is to <u>drink</u> as <u>hamburger</u> is to _____ .

14.   <u>Daisy</u> is to <u>flower</u> as <u>maple</u> is to _____ .

15.   <u>Car</u> is to <u>driver</u> as <u>plane</u> is to _____ .

16.   <u>Ceiling</u> is to <u>room</u> as <u>lid</u> is to _____ .

17.   <u>Paper</u> is to <u>tear</u> as <u>glass</u> is to _____ .

Make a list of five or six activities you like to do. Some examples are running, hopping, sit-ups, jumping jacks, touching your toes, push-ups, skipping rope, and playing sports. Write about how these activities help you stay healthy.

_____

_____

_____

_____

_____

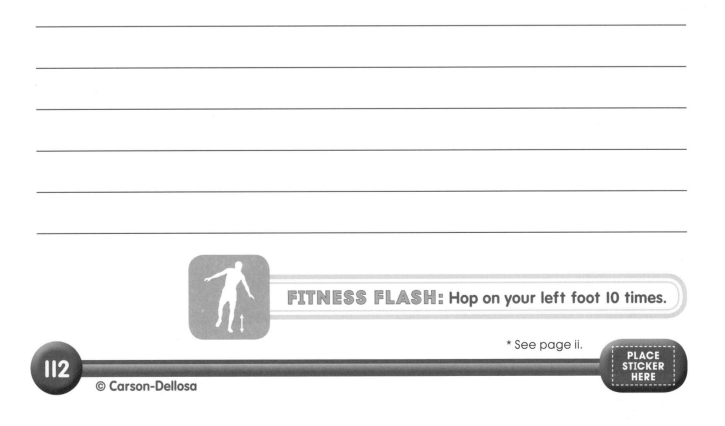

FITNESS FLASH: Hop on your left foot 10 times.

* See page ii.

PLACE STICKER HERE

Each sentence is missing a comma after an introductory phrase. Add the comma using this symbol: ⌄ .

1. Unfortunately the package did not arrive in time.

2. Although Hannah was near the front of the line she did not get to choose the book she wanted.

3. On Saturday Dad is going to make pancakes for breakfast.

4. At the corner of Wilcox Road and Pinevale Avenue there is a fruit stand.

5. Sadly we were not able to rescue the baby bird.

6. In spite of the rain the festival was a lot of fun.

7. To get to the pond take Dragonfly Trail.

8. First stretch your arms above your head as far as you can reach.

Follow the directions in order.

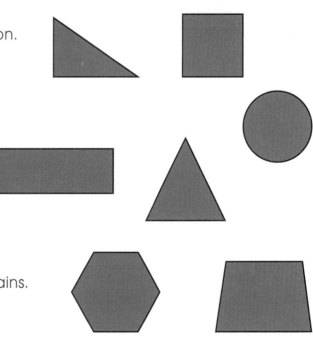

9. Cross out the figure that is not a polygon.

10. Cross out the regular quadrilateral.

11. Cross out the parallelogram.

12. Cross out the right triangle.

13. Cross out the hexagon.

14. Cross out the regular polygon.

15. Circle the name of the figure that remains.

    kite   trapezoid   rhombus

DAY 8

Read the story. Then, answer the questions that follow.

Who Did It?

Grayson and Dustin were playing volleyball in their backyard with some friends. They had been playing all afternoon in the hot sun. Dustin decided that he was tired of playing volleyball. He sat down on the back steps to watch the others. "I'm going into the house to get a drink of water," said Dustin. Several of the others decided that they were thirsty too, and they went inside with Dustin.

After getting a drink of water, the other boys headed home for dinner. Dustin told his brother that he was hungry and went to the kitchen for something to eat. Dustin's dad came into the kitchen to make dinner. "Who ate all of the hot dogs?" he exclaimed. "They were right here on the counter."

Grayson and Dustin looked at each other. "We didn't, Dad," Dustin said. Dad said, "Well, somebody must have. Do you have any clues?"

They all started looking around for clues. The boys' muddy shoes had left tracks on the floor, but the tracks weren't in the area where the hot dogs had been. Just then, everyone heard what sounded like a satisfied *meow* coming from the den. They rushed into the den just in time to see Tiger, Dustin's cat, gobbling down the last hot dog. Tiger licked his paws clean. "No wonder we didn't find any cat tracks in the kitchen," laughed Dustin's dad. "Tiger always keeps his paws very clean, unlike some boys I know."

16. Why weren't there any tracks in the area where the hot dogs had been?

     _____

17. From whose point of view is the story told? Do you think it is an effective point of view to use for this story? Explain.

     _____

     _____

18. On a separate sheet of paper, write an alternate final paragraph to the story with your own solution to the mystery.

PLACE STICKER HERE

Use the graph to answer each question.

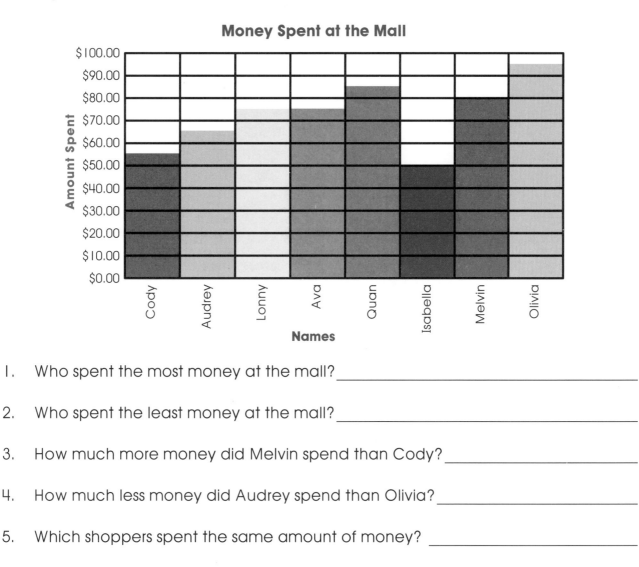

Money Spent at the Mall

1. Who spent the most money at the mall?_____

2. Who spent the least money at the mall?_____

3. How much more money did Melvin spend than Cody?_____

4. How much less money did Audrey spend than Olivia?_____

5. Which shoppers spent the same amount of money? _____

6. What was the average amount of money spent? To find the average, divide the total amount spent by the number of shoppers._____

Circle each root word. Underline each prefix.

7. unhappy   8. preheat   9. bicycle

10. review   11. misunderstand   12. unknown

13. uncover   14. uniform   15. replace

Solve each problem.

16. $409.75
    − 249.83
    $ _____ .

17. $14.74
    × 3
    $ _____ .

18. $492.00
    − 349.50
    $ _____ .

19. $ _____ .
    4)$12.92

20. $162.49
    + 186.32
    $ _____ .

21. $ _____ .
    7)$49.77

22. $601.89
    + 403.23
    $ _____ .

23. $9.57
    × 6
    $ _____ .

Use a print or online dictionary to find the definition for each word. Write the definition on the line.

24. anticipate _____

25. predicament _____

26. prominent _____

27. conspicuous _____

28. sanctuary _____

29. stifle _____

FITNESS FLASH: Do 10 jumping jacks.

Write the correct word to complete each sentence.

energy	food groups	Nutrients
Exercise	healthy	water

1. _____ are basic, nourishing ingredients in good foods that you eat.

2. _____ helps you strengthen your muscles, heart, and lungs.

3. Your body is between 55 and 75 percent _____ .

4. Meat, fruits, vegetables, milk, and breads and cereals make up the basic

   _____ .

5. Being healthy means feeling good and having the _____ to work and play.

6. Being _____ means feeling good and staying well.

Add both a prefix and a suffix to each word.

7. _____ print_____ 8. _____ port_____

9. _____ spell_____ 10. _____ courage _____

11. _____ light_____ 12. _____ cook_____

13. _____ lock_____ 14. _____ agree_____

Choose two of the new words and use them in sentences.

15. _____

16. _____

DAY 10

Mr. Mackle filled pots with different amounts of soil. Show the data on the line plot.

Container	A	B	C	D	E	F	G	H	I	J	K	L
Amounts of soil	$22\frac{1}{8}$ quarts	24 quarts	$22\frac{1}{2}$ quarts	$20\frac{1}{2}$ quarts	$22\frac{1}{8}$ quarts	$22\frac{1}{4}$ quarts	$22\frac{1}{2}$ quarts	$20\frac{1}{4}$ quarts	$22\frac{1}{2}$ quarts	$20\frac{1}{2}$ quarts	$22\frac{1}{4}$ quarts	24 quarts

Key
Pot of soil = X

$$20 \quad \frac{1}{2} \quad 21 \quad \frac{1}{2} \quad 22 \quad \frac{1}{2} \quad 23 \quad \frac{1}{2} \quad 24$$

If Mr. Mackle combined the soil from all the pots and redistributed it equally between all the pots, how much soil would each pot contain? _____

Series commas are missing from the sentences. Use the proofreading mark ⌄ to add commas where they are needed.

17. Mrs. Zheng planted zinnias cosmos poppies and bluebells in her wildflower garden.

18. This week, we have seen cardinals chickadees sparrows and robins at the feeder.

19. Darius invited Erik Joey Roberto and Sam to sleep over on Saturday.

20. Please remember to get broccoli cheddar cheese orange juice and bread at the grocery store.

21. Malia brought watercolors paintbrushes and a pad of paper to her art class.

22. Sadie won a goldfish a teddy bear and a plastic bracelet at the carnival.

CHARACTER CHECK: What is the hardest thing that you have ever done? How did it make you feel? On a separate sheet of paper, write a paragraph about your experience.

PLACE STICKER HERE

The *volume* of a rectangular solid is found by multiplying its length by its width by its height. The formula is *l* x *w* x *h*.

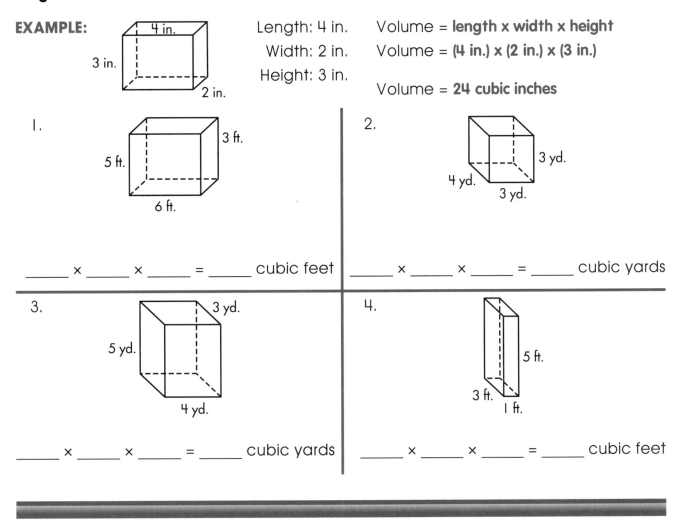

EXAMPLE:

Length: 4 in.   Volume = **length x width x height**
Width: 2 in.   Volume = **(4 in.) x (2 in.) x (3 in.)**
Height: 3 in.
                 Volume = **24 cubic inches**

1.

_____ x _____ x _____ = _____ cubic feet

2.

_____ x _____ x _____ = _____ cubic yards

3.

_____ x _____ x _____ = _____ cubic yards

4.

_____ x _____ x _____ = _____ cubic feet

The word *and* is often used too frequently in writing. Rewrite this run-on sentence, leaving out the word *and* as much as possible.

My friend and I visited Cardiff, Wales, and we learned that Cardiff is the capital and largest port of Wales and the city lies on the River Taff near the Bristol Channel and Cardiff is near the largest coal mines in Great Britain.

_____

_____

_____

Read the passage. Then, answer the questions.

Plant Parts

Plants have many parts. You can see some of them, but they have parts that you can't see, too. The plant begins with the root system underground. It sends out roots into the soil to gather water and minerals. The part of the plant that grows out of the ground is called the *stem*. The stem moves water and minerals from the soil into the leaves. The leaves use sunlight, air, water, and minerals to make food for the plant, which is then moved to other parts of the plant. The leaves also produce the oxygen we breathe. Some leaves have only broad, flat areas connected to the stems. Others have many leaflets, or slim, needle-like parts. Many plants have flowers on top of the stems. The petals of the flowers help attract bees and butterflies, which bring pollen from other flowers. The pollen helps flowers make new plants for the next year. Some plants bear fruit. New plants can grow from the seeds in the fruit.

5. What is the main idea of this passage?

   a. A plant's root system is underground.

   b. Plants have parts such as roots, leaves, and petals.

   c. Bees and butterflies like flowers.

6. What are leaflets? _____

7. What do leaves need to make food for the plant? _____

_____

8. How do the petals of a flower help the plant? _____

_____

_____

FACTOID: Benjamin Franklin started the first lending library.

Choose two fiction books—they can be titles you choose yourself, or they can be books from the Summer Reading List that begins on page ix in this book. On a separate sheet of paper, write several paragraphs explaining how the two main characters from the two books are alike and different. Use details from the books to support your points. Plan your writing below.

_____

_____

_____

_____

Fractions that have a denominator of 10 can also be written as decimals. Write each fraction and/or decimal.

EXAMPLE:

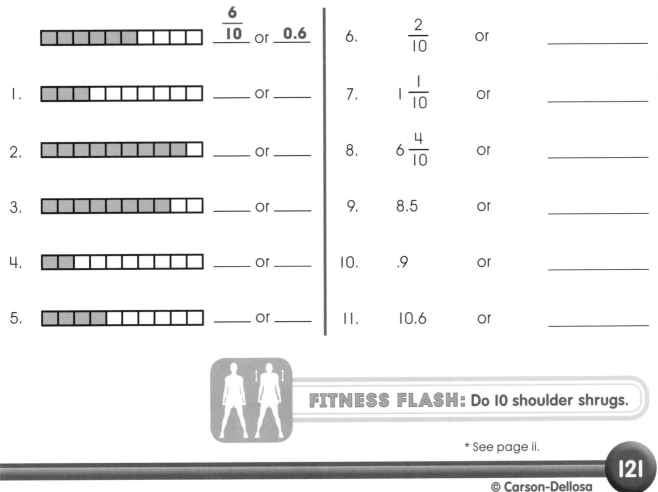

$\dfrac{6}{10}$ or **0.6**

6. $\dfrac{2}{10}$ or _____

7. $1\dfrac{1}{10}$ or _____

8. $6\dfrac{4}{10}$ or _____

9. 8.5 or _____

10. .9 or _____

11. 10.6 or _____

1. _____ or _____

2. _____ or _____

3. _____ or _____

4. _____ or _____

5. _____ or _____

FITNESS FLASH: Do 10 shoulder shrugs.

* See page ii.

DAY 12

Choose four idioms and draw a picture for each one.

- Could you lend a hand?
- The boys were shooting the breeze.
- She has a bee in her bonnet.
- She slept like a log.
- I got it straight from the horse's mouth.
- You won the game by the skin of your teeth.

- Time flies.
- Keep a stiff upper lip.
- She's a ball of fire.
- I'd really like to catch her eye.
- I was dog tired.

FITNESS FLASH: Jog in place for 30 seconds.

* See page ii.

PLACE STICKER HERE

Read each sentence. Then, circle the letter of the sentence in which the underlined word is used the same way it is in the first sentence.

1. Connor dropped a full pitcher of iced tea on the patio.
   A. Erin's best friend is the pitcher for the Wyattville Eagles.
   B. Jordan put the bouquet of tulips in the white ceramic pitcher.

2. Does Dad want ground coffee or whole-bean coffee?
   A. Julio cooked some ground turkey to put in the spaghetti sauce.
   B. The ground was wet for two days after the big storm on Tuesday.

3. Try not to pound too hard on the table.
   A. The recipe calls for one whole pound of butter!
   B. If you pound on the door, I'm sure I'll hear you.

4. The rest of the students will arrive in about an hour.
   A. Who ate the rest of the olives?
   B. "I want you to rest for half an hour before you go swimming," said Mom.

5. Emma and Miguel got engaged last night!
   A. The audience was engaged the moment Dr. Floss started performing the science experiments.
   B. Mom and Dad were engaged for two years before they got married.

Write the equivalent measurements.

6. 500 mm = _____ cm

7. 8 kg = _____ g

8. 6 L = _____ mL

9. 12,000 mL = _____ L

10. 8 m = _____ mm

11. 12 km = _____ m

12. 5 g = _____ mg

13. 17,000,000 mg = _____ kg

14. 4,000 L = _____ kL

15. 12 km = _____ m

16. 1 m = _____ cm

17. 1,000 m = _____ km

DAY 13

Read the passage. Then, answer the questions.

Climate

The climate describes the weather in an area over a long period of time. If you live somewhere where it rains a lot, then you live in a rainy climate. If your town is very hot and dry, then you may live in a desert climate. Some cities, such as San Diego, California, have a very mild climate. Others, such as New Orleans, Louisiana, have warm, heavy air, so it is humid most of the time. Although the weather in a place may change from day to day, a region's climate seldom changes. Factors other than weather can also affect the climate. Areas that are close to the sea tend to be cooler and wetter. They may also be cloudy because clouds form when warm inland air meets the cooler air from the sea. Mountains may also affect climate. Because the temperature at the top of a mountain is cooler than at ground level, it may snow year-round. Regions near Earth's equator, or middle, are warmer than those at the poles. Sunlight must travel farther to get to the north and south poles, so these areas are much colder.

18. What is the main idea of this passage?

    a. Climate is the weather in a place over a long period of time.

    b. The north and south poles are very cold.

    c. Some climates are rainy, and some are very hot.

19. How are the climates in San Diego and New Orleans different? _____

    _____

20. What is the difference between weather and climate? _____

    _____

21. How are climates near the equator different from those at the poles? _____

    _____

FACTOID: Recycling a ton of paper saves about 24 trees.

PLACE STICKER HERE

On the line, write the correct present-tense form of the verb in parentheses.

1. Bob _____ to the market to buy some lemonade for the party. (run)

2. Troy easily _____ the ball. (catch)

3. He _____ to the new school down the street. (go)

On the line, write the correct past-tense form of the verb in parentheses.

4. Julio _____ into the water from the diving board. (dive)

5. Angelo _____ his stepmother this week. (visit)

6. Ebony _____ to the movies yesterday with Drew and Lexi. (go)

On the line, write the correct future-tense form of the verb in parentheses.

7. Chiara _____ her new book this evening. (read)

8. Lauren _____ me her bracelet when she returns. (show)

9. Davion _____ both dogs this afternoon. (wash)

Write your favorite folktale. Tell how the story begins, what happens in the middle, and how it ends. Write it in your own words and in the correct order.

_____

_____

_____

_____

_____

_____

_____

DAY 14

Read the passage. Then, answer the questions.

Biofuels

Gasoline is used in cars, and oil is used to heat many homes. Biofuels have similar uses, but they are made from things like vegetable oil, which can be recycled and used again. Diesel is a type of fuel similar to heating oil. Diesel fuel is used in some cars and trucks. Biodiesel, most of which is made from soybean oil, burns more cleanly than diesel. It can be used in diesel engines without having to add any special parts. Biodiesel produces less pollution, so it is better for the environment. Gasoline is known as a fossil fuel, which means it comes from layers deep inside the earth that are made up of plants and animals that lived millions of years ago. Biofuel comes from plants we grow today, so it is a renewable resource. Some biofuels are created from restaurants' leftover oil that was used to cook french fries or fried chicken. Instead of throwing the oil away, some people are using it to run their cars!

10. What is the main idea of this passage?

    a. Biofuels are better for the environment than fossil fuels.

    b. Gasoline and diesel are used to run cars.

    c. Some people throw away the oil they have used for cooking.

11. What are biofuels? _____

    _____

12. Give two details from the passage that the author uses to support the main idea.

    _____

    _____

FITNESS FLASH: Hop on your right foot for 30 seconds.

* See page ii.

PLACE STICKER HERE

Plot the given points on the grid. Label each point.

A (2, 8)

B (3, 5)

C (7, 1)

D (4, 8)

E (5, 5)

F (1, 9)

G (9, 10)

H (6, 6)

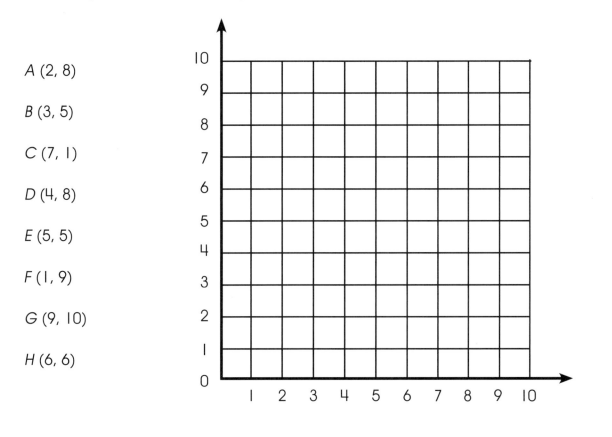

Read each sentence. On the line, write _S_ if it contains a simile, _M_ if it contains a metaphor, and _P_ if it contains personification.

1. _____ The girls were pieces of popcorn bouncing on the trampoline.

2. _____ Josiah was as still as a statue while Miss Denise cut his hair.

3. _____ The thunderstorm was a freight train rumbling through the night.

4. _____ The birds' tracks looked like scribbles in the snow.

5. _____ The friendly face of the moon winked at me through the trees.

6. _____ The blazing sun cooked the dry, brown earth.

7. _____ The raindrops playfully tickled the back of my neck.

Read the passage. Then, answer the questions.

Citizens' Rights and Responsibilities

In Canada and the United States, citizens have certain rights. These rights are often a part of the country's laws. American and Canadian citizens who are age 18 and over are given the right to vote. Citizens of the United States and Canada also have the right to a fair trial and the right to speak freely about what they believe. They can practice any religion they want to, and they have the right to gather peacefully to exchange ideas. They have the right to ask their government to change laws that they think are wrong. With these rights come responsibilities, too. People should obey the laws of their country. They should respect the opinions of others, even if they disagree with them. They should help others in their community and try to protect their environment. It is important to remember that all citizens are a part of a large community and that everyone deserves to be treated fairly.

8.   What is the main idea of this passage?

   a.   All citizens of a country have rights and responsibilities.

   b.   Citizens have the right to vote.

   c.   Everyone should be treated fairly in a community.

9.   What are three responsibilities citizens have? _____

_____

10.   At least how old must citizens be to vote in Canada and the United States?

_____

11.   What are three rights that citizens have in Canada and the United States?

_____

_____

FACTOID: An ostrich's eye is bigger than its brain.

Multiply dollar amounts like whole numbers. Then, the decimal point is inserted two numbers from the right to show cents. Multiply to find each product.

EXAMPLE:

$$\begin{array}{r} \$0.24 \\ \times\ \ 89 \\ \hline 216 \\ +\ 1920 \\ \hline 2136 \end{array}$$

$24 \times 9 = 216$

$24 \times 80 = 1920$

$1920 + 216 = 2136$

Place the decimal and dollar sign: **$21.36**

1.	2.	3.	4.
$0.65 × 24	$0.52 × 36	$0.94 × 13	$0.45 × 25

5.	6.	7.	8.
$0.81 × 34	$0.59 × 54	$3.52 × 34	$3.45 × 56

Underline the person being addressed in each sentence.

9. "Walter, you must clean your room today."

10. "I've been waiting for your call, Gerald, since you left two hours ago."

11. "Eli and Tanesha went to the park, Alejandro."

12. "I'm going to watch the movie, Ian."

13. "My room is clean and my homework is done, Dad."

14. "This artwork is exceptional, Betsy."

15. "Since you have been so helpful, Donna, you can call a friend."

16. "Tara, your story is very interesting."

DAY 16

To find the volume of a rectangular solid, multiply the length, width, and height of the solid. Find the volume of each figure.

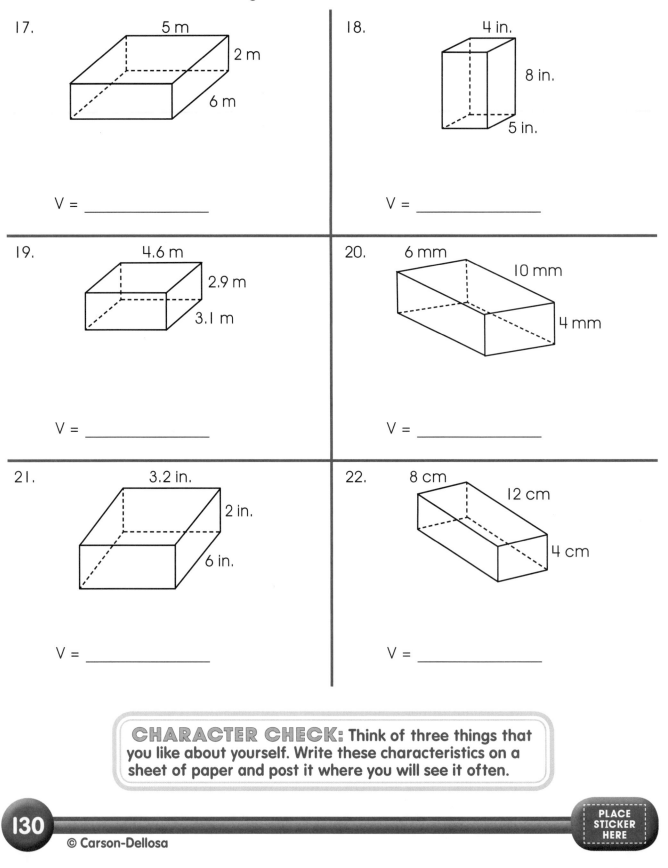

17. 5 m 2 m 6 m

V = _____

18. 4 in. 8 in. 5 in.

V = _____

19. 4.6 m 2.9 m 3.1 m

V = _____

20. 6 mm 10 mm 4 mm

V = _____

21. 3.2 in. 2 in. 6 in.

V = _____

22. 8 cm 12 cm 4 cm

V = _____

CHARACTER CHECK: Think of three things that you like about yourself. Write these characteristics on a sheet of paper and post it where you will see it often.

PLACE STICKER HERE

Loyalty Lunch

Loyalty means to support and stand up for the people you love. Think of the characteristics that make a person loyal. Then, design a menu for a loyalty lunch to share with a friend or family member. Think of a special name that uses a characteristic of loyalty for each food item, such as Dependable Diced Tomatoes or Honest Olives. Gather some ingredients for the meal. Use folded index cards to make place cards and labels that tell what each food is. As you eat, talk to your dining partner about why you appreciate his loyal friendship.

Multiply fractions to solve each problem. Write answers in simplest form.

1. Isabel mailed 8 packages at the post office. Each package weighed $\frac{3}{4}$ pound. What was the total weight of all 8 packages?

_____ pounds

2. A single serving of tuna casserole requires $\frac{1}{8}$ cup of bread crumbs. How many cups of bread crumbs are needed for 12 servings?

_____ cups

3. Carlos stacked 11 bricks. If each brick was $\frac{2}{5}$ foot tall, how tall was the stack?

_____ feet

4. Clark's school is $\frac{7}{8}$ mile from his house. If he has walked $\frac{3}{4}$ of the way to school, how far has he walked?

_____ mile

DAY 17

Think of someone who is brave. It can be a person you know, someone famous, or someone from history. Write a paragraph describing this person and explaining how he or she shows bravery.

_____

_____

_____

_____

_____

1 pint (pt.) is equal to 2 cups.	1 gallon (gal.) is equal to 4 quarts.
1 quart (qt.) is equal to 2 pints.	1 pound (lb.) is equal to 16 ounces.

Circle the best answer.

5.	The capacity of a glass	2 cups	2 pt.	2 qt.	2 gal.
6.	The capacity of a bathtub	60 cups	60 pt.	60 qt.	60 gal.
7.	The capacity of a kitchen sink	2 cups	2 pt.	2 qt.	2 gal.

Convert each measurement.

8. 5 pt. = _____ cups   9. 4 pt. = _____ qt.   10. 2 qt. = _____ pt.

11. 32 oz. = _____ lb.   12. 3 gal. = _____ qt.   13. 8 cups = _____ pt.

FITNESS FLASH: Hop on your left foot 10 times.

* See page ii.

PLACE STICKER HERE

132

Write each decimal number in standard form.

1. $(5 \times 10{,}000) + (5 \times 1{,}000) + (3 \times 100) + (6 \times 10) + (4 \times 1) + (9 \times \frac{1}{10})$ _____

2. $(4 \times 100) + (7 \times 10) + (6 \times 1) + (8 \times \frac{1}{10}) + (2 \times \frac{1}{100})$ _____

3. $(2 \times 100{,}000) + (8 \times 1{,}000) + (3 \times 10) + (6 \times 1) + (4 \times \frac{1}{10}) + (8 \times \frac{1}{1{,}000})$ _____

4. $(2 \times 1{,}000) + (1 \times 100) + (1 \times 1) + (5 \times \frac{1}{10}) + (3 \times \frac{1}{100}) + (6 \times \frac{1}{1{,}000})$ _____

5. $(4 \times 400{,}000) + (2 \times 100) + (5 \times 10) + (8 \times \frac{1}{100}) + (6 \times \frac{1}{1{,}000})$ _____

6. $(3 \times 10{,}000{,}000) + (7 \times 1{,}000{,}000) + (2 \times 100) + (5 \times 1) + (1 \times \frac{1}{10}) + (1 \times \frac{1}{100}) +$

   $(1 \times \frac{1}{1{,}000})$ _____

Write each number in expanded form.

7. 126,552.254 _____

8. 7,520,634.48 _____

An event can cause another event to happen. A clue word can help you find out which is the cause and which is the effect. In each sentence, underline the cause with a straight line (___) and underline the effect with a dashed line (____). Draw a box around each clue word.

EXAMPLE: The flowers were very bright, so they attracted a lot of butterflies.

9. The book was ripped because the dog chewed it.

10. Because it was so cold, Betty could ice-skate for only a short while.

11. I went to bed early last night because I was so tired.

12. Because it was raining hard, we couldn't play outside.

13. The rabbit ran away quickly because it saw a cat.

14. It was very foggy outside, so we could not see the mountains.

15. Because we got to the camp too late, there was no time for hiking.

Read the passage. Then, answer the questions.

The Economy

You may have heard your family or a newscaster discuss the economy. The economy is a system in which goods and services are exchanged for money. Goods are items that are produced, such as books and clothing. Services are activities that people do for each other. For example, a teacher provides the service of educating students, and a police officer provides the service of keeping the community safe. Sometimes people provide a service that produces a good, such as a chef who prepares a meal. People pay money for goods and services. When you pay a producer of goods, she can use the money to purchase the materials to make more goods. When you pay a service provider, he can use the money to pay for more training so that he can do his job even better. Providers also use the money to pay for basic items such as food and shelter. When newscasters report that the economy is strong, it means that most people are happy with the amount of money, goods, and services they have.

16. What is the main idea of this passage?

    a. Newscasters often talk about the economy.

    b. Sometimes the economy is strong, and other times it is weak.

    c. The economy is a system in which goods and services are exchanged for money.

17. What are goods? _____

18. List two examples of goods. _____

19. What are services? _____

20. List two examples of service providers. _____

_____

FACTOID: Camels have three sets of eyelids to protect their eyes from sand.

PLACE STICKER HERE

Complete the graph using the information in the table.

Day	High Temperature (°F)
Monday	87°
Tuesday	90°
Wednesday	74°
Thursday	78°
Friday	80°

Highest Temperature

Temperature

90°
88°
86°
84°
82°
80°
78°
76°
74°

M   T   W   Th   F

Days of the Week

Put on Your Dancing Shoes!

To boost your endurance, you have to push yourself so that your heart beats faster and you breathe harder. Dancing can be one of the most enjoyable ways to build your endurance, and it may not feel like exercise! Find an open area where you can move to your favorite upbeat tunes. Start by dancing continuously for 10 minutes several times per week. You do not need any dance training; simply move to the music's beat. Gradually increase the length of each dance time for an even better aerobic workout. Dancing is not only good for endurance, but it can also improve your mood, decrease anxiety, improve sleep, relieve stress, and raise self-esteem.

* See page ii.

DAY 19

> ***Point of view* refers to the person who is telling the story or who is "speaking."**
> A story can be told from three different points of view:
> * In first person, the main character tells the story.
> * In second person, the story is told as though it is happening to you.
> * In third person, a narrator tells the story as if she is watching it happen.

Read each story and circle the point of view.

1. Marcus's family had just moved to a large city from a very small town. He was surprised at how many cars were on the street and how few people said hello when he met them on the sidewalk. In his old town, he had known everyone. He hoped that he would make a new friend on the first day of school. When he saw the crowded hallways, he felt worried. Then, he thought to himself that with all of those people around, he was sure to make a lot of friends.

       First Person   **Second Person**   **Third Person**

2. When my family moved to the big city, I was excited about all of the new activities we could try. I never thought how crowded it might be. Back home, my neighbors were friendly. It seemed like I knew everyone in the whole town. I wanted to make new friends in the city, but when I got to school, the hallways were so packed that I could hardly get to my classroom. I took a deep breath and said to myself, "With all of these people around, I am sure to make new friends!"

       First Person   **Second Person**   **Third Person**

3. You and your family have just moved to the city. You are surprised to see so many cars on the road. In your old town, you felt like you knew everyone. When you drive up to the school, your mother wishes you good luck. You walk into the building and start to look for your classroom. You think to yourself that with all of these people around, you are sure to make some new friends.

       First Person   **Second Person**   **Third Person**

FITNESS FLASH: Do 10 jumping jacks.

* See page ii.

PLACE STICKER HERE

Circle a homophone in the puzzle for each word in the word bank. For example, if the word in the word bank is *ant*, you would look for its homophone *aunt* in the puzzle. Words can go across and down.

allowed	nose	Greece	brews	hole
sighs	ate	threw	bored	
gene	serial	hare	seam	

```
i  a  l  o  u  d  b  e  t  i  c  a  l  s  e  e  m  u  r  a  s
u  d  m  n  a  j  k  n  a  c  c  e  t  t  o  h  q  h  k  e  i
o  j  e  a  n  e  l  o  c  s  i  y  h  m  n  u  s  a  x  d  z
j  e  m  u  p  r  e  k  i  x  u  p  r  b  s  i  u  i  m  p  e
f  c  q  n  r  i  m  n  t  c  o  e  o  n  o  w  f  r  r  h  e
b  t  k  s  o  b  g  o  o  d  c  x  u  k  n  h  f  t  q  w  a
a  i  v  s  n  r  r  w  x  i  g  z  g  j  a  o  i  v  e  r  b
b  o  a  r  d  u  b  s  d  v  r  r  h  s  n  l  x  o  x  f  k
r  e  l  s  u  i  s  d  c  u  e  p  l  d  t  e  o  h  j  i  c
y  s  j  i  n  s  q  w  m  y  a  s  e  p  b  g  p  i  u  n  l
k  m  c  e  r  e  a  l  g  u  s  a  r  h  e  i  g  h  t  y  g
o  t  j  q  e  w  a  z  x  s  e  e  d  c  v  f  r  t  g  b  n
```

FACTOID: The amount of water pouring over Niagara Falls each second could fill 13,000 bathtubs.

Read the passage. Then, answer the questions.

City Services

Cities provide many services to the people who live there. The mayor and city council, who are elected by the citizens of a city, make the laws that everyone must follow. They also meet to discuss community issues, such as whether to build a new recreation center. Other city employees include police officers and firefighters. These people work to keep everyone in the city safe. Other city services include the library, where the public can check out books, and companies that provide water and electricity. Some cities have special programs for the people who live there, such as reading clubs at the library or computer classes for senior citizens. It takes many services to make a city work. Some people like to give back to their communities by doing volunteer work. They might teach swimming lessons or offer to pick up litter in the parks. When everyone in a city works together, it can be a great place to live.

I.   What is the main idea of this passage?

    a.   People living in a city receive many services.

    b.   Some people like to give back to their communities.

    c.   A library is a place where people can check out books.

2.   Who elects the mayor and the city council? _____

_____

3.   What do the mayor and city council members do? _____

_____

4.   Name three employees who work for the city. _____

_____

CHARACTER CHECK: Think of something that upsets you. How might you show tolerance toward it?

PLACE STICKER HERE

Global Climates

Climate is the pattern of weather that occurs in a certain area over a long period of time. In this experiment, you will see why certain areas of the earth have different climates and temperatures.

Materials:
- adjustable gooseneck lamp
- 2 thermometers
- ruler
- globe
- duct tape
- timer or clock

Procedure:

1. Position the lamp about one foot (30 cm) from the globe. Because Earth is tilted on its axis (23.5°), position the globe so that the northern hemisphere is tilted away from the lamp. In this position, the northern hemisphere is experiencing winter.

2. On the side of the globe nearest the lamp, use two small pieces of duct tape to attach one thermometer over the equator and the other thermometer near the north pole.

3. Record the initial temperature at each location in the table below.

4. Turn on the lamp. Record the temperatures again after five minutes.

Reading	North Pole	Equator
Initial temperature (°F)		
Temperature after five minutes (°F)		

Conclusions:
Answer the questions on a separate sheet of paper.

1. Was there a difference between the initial and final temperatures? Why?

2. What was the difference in the final temperature between the north pole and the equator? Give an explanation for your results.

3. What if you positioned the globe so that the northern hemisphere was tilted toward the lamp? Predict how the temperature at the north pole might be different. Then, conduct an experiment to test your prediction.

4. How does this explain the process that causes different climates on Earth?

BONUS

Solar and Lunar Eclipses

An eclipse can occur when the light of the sun becomes blocked by the moon or Earth. Two types of shadows can be observed during an eclipse: an umbra and a penumbra. The umbra is the darkest part of a shadow. If you are standing in the umbra, the source of light is completely blocked by the object causing the shadow. This is different from the penumbra, in which the light source is only partially blocked, and there is only a partial shadow.

Procedure:

1. Use a ruler to draw two straight lines from point **A** on the sun through points **C** and **D** on the moon. Stop the lines when they strike the edge of Earth.

2. Draw two additional straight lines from point **B** on the sun through points **C** and **D** on the moon. Stop the lines when they strike the edge of Earth.

3. Use a colorful pencil to shade in the **umbra**. Using a different color, shade in the **penumbra**. Show what colors you used in the key.

Conclusions:

Answer the questions on a separate sheet of paper.

1. Name the type of eclipse pictured in the diagram.

2. During which phase of the moon would this type of eclipse occur?

3. If you were observing this eclipse from Earth, in which part of the shadow would you need to be to observe a total eclipse?

4. With an adult, use the Internet to find out when you may be able to view this type of eclipse.

Chile

Use the graph to answer the questions.

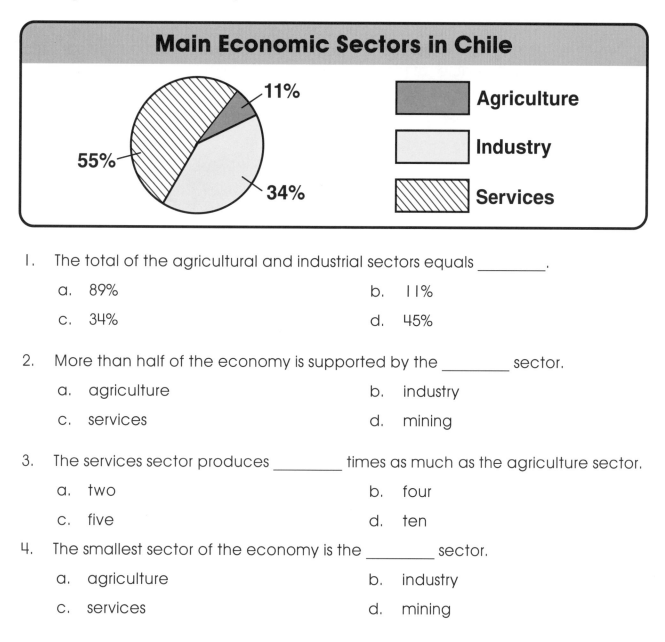

Main Economic Sectors in Chile

11%

55%

34%

Agriculture

Industry

Services

1. The total of the agricultural and industrial sectors equals _____.

   a. 89%   b. 11%

   c. 34%   d. 45%

2. More than half of the economy is supported by the _____ sector.

   a. agriculture   b. industry

   c. services   d. mining

3. The services sector produces _____ times as much as the agriculture sector.

   a. two   b. four

   c. five   d. ten

4. The smallest sector of the economy is the _____ sector.

   a. agriculture   b. industry

   c. services   d. mining

BONUS

Deforestation

Deforestation is the cutting down, burning, and damaging of forests. In Brazil, this refers to the tropical rain forest called the *Amazon*. Forests are cut for agricultural purposes, such as planting crops or grazing cattle, as well as for commercial logging. The problems resulting from deforestation include an increase in global warming and the extinction of many species of plants and animals. The government of Brazil has used several programs to preserve the remaining rain forests, but many people are still concerned over the continued destruction of the Amazon rain forest.

Use the chart to answer the questions.

Rate of Deforestation in Brazil	
Years	**Square Kilometers**
2005–2006	14,285
2006–2007	11,651
2007–2008	12,911
2008–2009	7,464
2009–2010	7,000
2010–2011	6,418
2011–2012	4,571
2012–2013	5,891

1. The smallest amount of deforestation took place between _____.

   a. 2005–2006   b. 2010–2011   c. 2008–2009   d. 2011–2012

2. More deforestation took place between 2008 and 2009 than between _____.

   a. 2007–2008   b. 2009–2010   c. 2006–2007   d. 2005–2006

3. Between 2010 and 2012, what was the decrease in square kilometers of deforestation?

   a. 10,989   b. 1,847   c. 1,320   d. 2,634

South American Time Line

Use the time line to answer the questions.

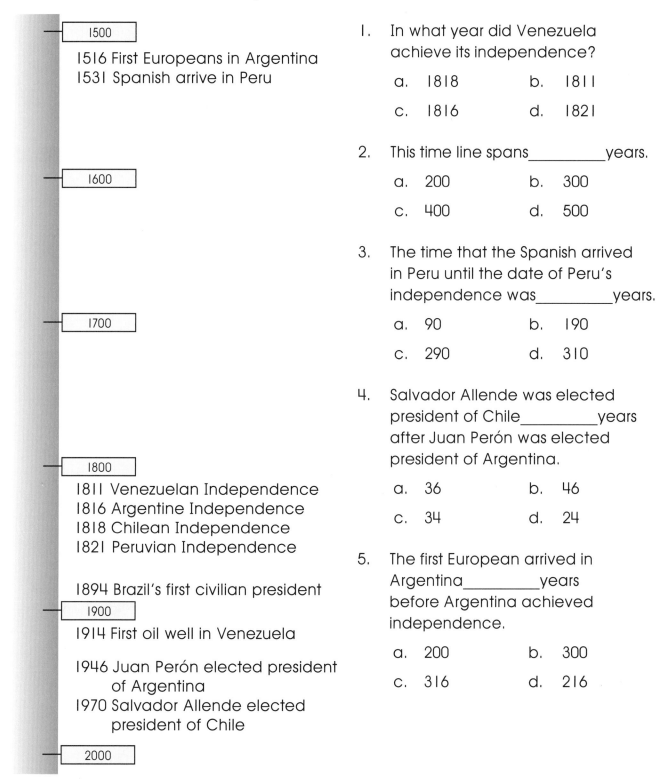

1500

1516 First Europeans in Argentina
1531 Spanish arrive in Peru

1600

1700

1800

1811 Venezuelan Independence
1816 Argentine Independence
1818 Chilean Independence
1821 Peruvian Independence

1894 Brazil's first civilian president

1900

1914 First oil well in Venezuela

1946 Juan Perón elected president
of Argentina
1970 Salvador Allende elected
president of Chile

2000

1. In what year did Venezuela achieve its independence?
   a. 1818   b. 1811
   c. 1816   d. 1821

2. This time line spans_____years.
   a. 200   b. 300
   c. 400   d. 500

3. The time that the Spanish arrived in Peru until the date of Peru's independence was_____years.
   a. 90   b. 190
   c. 290   d. 310

4. Salvador Allende was elected president of Chile_____years after Juan Perón was elected president of Argentina.
   a. 36   b. 46
   c. 34   d. 24

5. The first European arrived in Argentina_____years before Argentina achieved independence.
   a. 200   b. 300
   c. 316   d. 216

Take It Outside!

Invite a friend or family member to join you outside for a picnic. Pack foods that must be divided into pieces or sections, like oranges, sandwiches, and pizza. When you arrive at your eating spot, explain that this is a percentage picnic. As you share each item, cut out the portions and point out the percentages of items that you are eating. For example, you may give your friend 25 percent of an orange, but he might only eat 50 percent of the portion.

During the summer, nature provides wonderful inspiration for art. Seek and capture an outdoor image or scene that you find extraordinary. For example, you may find the combination of colors the moment before the sun sets to be inspiring. Use a variety of art materials, such as torn paper, fabric swatches, wallpaper scraps, glue, markers, and foam board, to design a three-dimensional piece of artwork that shows the qualities of the scene.

The characteristics of many plants and animals are inherited. However, the characteristics of some plants and animals change as a result of their environments. These changes are called *adaptations*. With an adult, go online or visit the library to learn more about the plants and animals that live near you. Then, go on a nature walk. Look for plants and animals that you read about, such as birds, insects, and flowers, and observe them. As you observe them, think about how each plant or animal adapted to survive in its environment.

Write a letter to a friend or relative, sharing what you learned about local plants and animals and their adaptations. If your friend or relative lives out of town, ask him or her to tell you about the local plants or animals there.

* See page ii.

Section I

Day 1/Page 3: 1. 8; 2. 6; 3. 12; 4. 11; 5. 5; 6. 10; 7. 30; 8. 5; 9. 18; 10. 8; 11. 18; 12. 9; 13. 3; 14. 9; 15. 13; 16. 6; 17. 7; 18. 8; 19. 7; 20. 24; 21. 0; 22. yes; 23. yes; 24. yes; 25. no; 26. no; 27. yes; 28. yes; 29. yes; 30. no; 31. no; 32. no; 33. no; 34. enemy; 35. time; 36. overlook; 37. sky

Day 2/Page 5: 1. "I love going to the natural history museum!" exclaimed Ananya.; 2. "I usually go see the animals first," replied Noah, "and then I go to the planetarium."; 3. "Have you seen the dinosaur fossils?" asked Eliza.; 4. She added, "The dioramas of prehistoric life are really cool."; 5. "That's my favorite part," said Antonio.; 6. "Did you know that I'm one-quarter Native American?" asked Dylan.; 7. "That's why I like the display of Native American artifacts," he said.; 8. "Let's start out with the western life display," suggested Mira, "and then head over to the planetarium."; 9. 1 × 16, 2 × 8, 4 × 4; 10. 1 × 15, 3 × 5; 11. 1 × 36, 2 × 18, 3 × 12, 4 × 9, 6 × 6; 12. 1 × 42, 2 × 21, 3 × 14, 6 × 7; 13. 1 × 24, 2 × 12, 3 × 8, 4 × 6; 14. 1 × 99, 3 × 33, 9 × 11; 15. 500 years; 16. 274 feet (83 m); 17. The weather turned colder and people trampled the ground near the trees' roots.; 18. warmth and water; 19. The author supports the statement that not many sequoias are alive today by explaining that they need warmer air to live and that their roots have a hard time absorbing water in hard ground.

Day 3/Page 7: 1. 90 − 10 = 80; 2. 100 − 10 = 90; 3. 90 − 40 = 50; 4. 900 − 600 = 300; 5. 60 − 40 = 20; 6. 20 + 40 = 60; 7. 200 + 200 = 400; 8. 60 + 40 = 100; 9. who; 10. who; 11. that; 12. which; 13. which; 14. that; 15. whose; 16. that; 17. Answers will vary.; 18. Answers will vary.;

A. 3:00; B. 9:00; C. 3:30; 19. 3:50 P.M.; 20. 3:00 A.M.; 21. 8:35 A.M.; 22. 3:00 A.M.; 23. 5:05 A.M.; 24. 5 hours, 30 minutes; 25. Natalia missed the bus, so her stepdad drove her to school.; 26. The male cardinal landed on the feeder, and its mate joined it a moment later.; 27. Ian is going ice-skating on Saturday, and Abby is going to a birthday party.; 28. We planned to cook out tonight, but it looks like it's going to storm.; 29. Xander has a lot of homework, so we're not going to the movies.; 30. The deer crossed the road, and her two fawns followed.

Day 4/Page 9: Patterns will vary.; Mr. Greg Jones, 1461 Condor St., Lake Tona, OH 98562; 1. b; 2. the study of stars, planets, and the universe; 3. to see stars and to measure their distance from Earth and their speed; 4. when certain objects will appear in the sky; 5. Answers will vary. Possible answer: The firsthand account would be in first person point of view. It might tell fascinating real-life stories about being an astronomer. I would rather read the firsthand account because it would be more real and interesting.

Day 5/Page 11: Answers will vary. Possible answers: 1. I will be walking to school.; 2. I am reading a kids' nature magazine.; 3. I will be eating leftover lasagna.; 4. I was watching a movie called *Matilda*.; 5.–6. Answers will vary.; 7. 309; 8. 8,846; 9. 296; 10. 322; 11. 3,991; 12. 132; 13. 362; 14. 826; 15. there; 16. their; 17. their; 18. there; 19. there; 20.–21. Answers will vary.

Day 6/Page 13: 1. smallest; 2. loudest; 3. shortest; 4. fastest; 5. happiest; 6. biggest; 7.–11. Answers will vary.; 12. four striped beach balls; 13. antique seagrass basket; 14. yellow ceramic mug;

15. rough gray rock; 16. six small red plastic trucks; 17. plump juicy tomato; 18. stray white dog; 19. 12, 11, Add three, subtract one.; 20. 29, 37, Increase the addend by one each time; 21. 42, 68, Add two previous numbers.

Day 7/Page 15: 1. $\frac{14}{10}$ or $1\frac{2}{5}$; 2. $\frac{8}{4}$ or 2; 3. $\frac{11}{11}$ or 1; 4. $\frac{24}{12}$ or 2; 5. $\frac{13}{11}$ or $1\frac{2}{11}$; 6. $\frac{15}{12}$ or $1\frac{1}{4}$; 7. $\frac{11}{8}$ or $1\frac{3}{8}$; 8. $\frac{15}{15}$ or 1; 9. $\frac{18}{16}$ or $1\frac{1}{8}$; 10. $\frac{9}{7}$ or $1\frac{2}{7}$; 11. $\frac{14}{9}$ or $1\frac{5}{9}$; Students' writing will vary.; 12. a.; 13. Answers may include lizards, snakes, turtles, crocodiles and frogs, toads, salamanders.; 14. Organizing the passage as a comparison works well because reptiles and amphibians are similar but not exactly alike.

Day 8/Page 17:

The total weight of all the potatoes is 5 pounds.; The difference in weight is $\frac{1}{2}$ pound.; 1. **had**, finished; 2. **have**, enjoyed; 3. **were**, cleaning; 4. **have been**, sleeping; Answers will vary, but may include: 5. was; 6. was; 7. am; 8. were; 9. pre; 10. dis; 11. re; 12. tri; 13. uni; 14. re; 15. un; 16. bi; 17. This metaphor means that your smile is cheerful.; 18. This metaphor means that winning the award was amazing.; 19. This metaphor means that the store is confusing to walk through.; 20. This metaphor means that the pillow was soft.

Day 9/Page 19: 1. 2 nickels, 1 penny; 2. 1 dime, 1 nickel, 5 pennies; 3. 1 quarter, 1 dime, 2 nickels, 2 pennies; 4. 1 quarter, 2 nickels, 1 dime; 5. 3 nickels, 2 pennies; 6. 2 dimes, 4 nickels; 7. why; 8. where; 9. why; 10. where;

11. when; 12. where; 13. when; 14. why; 15. Answers will vary. Possible answer: *Pit, pat, patter, clatter* sounds like the noise the rain makes. Using onomatopoeia makes the poem come to life.; 16. Answers will vary. Possible answer: smiling flower; 17. AABB; 18. Answers will vary. Possible answer: The poet feels joyous and excited about the coming of spring. She uses exclamation points and words like *shining, bursting, smiling,* and *pride*.

Day 10/Page 21: 1. <u>uni</u>corn; 2. <u>geo</u>logy; 3. speed<u>ometer</u>; 4. <u>aqua</u>rium; 5. <u>dentist</u>ry; 6. <u>fract</u>ure; 7. 18; 8. 11; 9. 63; 10. 32; 11. 28; 12. 81; 13. 5; 14. 24; 15. 40; 16. 21; 17. 9; 18. 2; 19. 24; 20. 18; 21. 25; 22. 45; 23. 54; 24. 56; 25. 64; 26. 7; 27. 49; Students should circle the products for numbers 8., 13., 18., and 26. because they are prime.; Answers and drawings will vary.; Answers will vary. Possible answers: 28. beside her brother; 29. in a pan; 30. to the top; 31. at Shea Stadium; 32. onto the floor; 33. at the grocery store; 34. in the air; 35. beneath a large branch

Day 11/Page 23: 1.–6. Parallel lines should be drawn.; 7.–16. Answers will vary.; 17. bridge; 18. country; 19. city; 20. person; 21. ocean; 22. landmark; 23. month; 24. person; 25. 2,740; 26. 114; 27. 11,109; 28. 5,034; 29. 70; 30. 131 R2; 31. 367 R4; 32. 1,274; 33. Kenya got a haircut. She really liked the way it looked.; 34. The rabbit hopped across the yard. It ran into the bushes.; 35. Molly helped Dad weed the garden. Then, they played in the sprinkler.

Day 12/Page 25: 1. 3,983; 2. 11,701; 3. 30,388; 4. 31,731; 5. 21,701; 6. 12,293; 7. 8,667; 8. 10,354; 45°, 65°, 110°; 45° + 65° = 110°; 9. >; 10. =; 11. <; 12. <; 13. >; 14. =; 15. >; 16. >; 17. <; 18. <; 19.

>; 20. >; 21. <; 22. <; Because they are smart "kids"!; 23. point; 24. ray; 25. line segment; 26. parallel lines; 27. line; 28. perpendicular lines

Day 13/Page 27: Stories will vary.; 1. 1, 0; 2. 2, 4; 3. 2, 0; 4. 0, 1; 5. a; 6. popular government, or government by the people; 7. People vote on every decision.; 8. People elect leaders who represent their viewpoints and vote on the issues.

Day 14/Page 29: 1. antonym; 2. mountain; 3. approximate; 4. renewable; 5. believe; 6. tutor; 7. $\frac{7}{8}$, Students should shade $\frac{7}{8}$.; 8. $\frac{5}{7}$, Students should shade $\frac{5}{7}$.; 9. $\frac{8}{10}$, Students should shade $\frac{8}{10}$.; 10. $\frac{4}{5}$, Students should shade $\frac{4}{5}$.; 11. 9 square cm; 12. 12 square cm; 13. $11\frac{1}{2}$ cm; 14. $8\frac{1}{2}$ cm; 15. $\frac{3}{4} + \frac{1}{4} + \frac{1}{4} = \frac{5}{4} = 1\frac{1}{4}$, $2 - 1\frac{1}{4} = \frac{3}{4}$ hour; 16. $\frac{2}{3} + \frac{1}{3} + \frac{2}{3} = \frac{5}{3} = 1\frac{2}{3}$ miles; 17. $\frac{5}{8} + \frac{1}{8} + \frac{1}{8} + \frac{1}{8} + \frac{1}{8} = \frac{9}{8} = 1\frac{1}{8}$ pounds; 18. $\frac{3}{16} + \frac{7}{16} = \frac{10}{16}$, $\frac{16}{16} - \frac{10}{16} = \frac{6}{16}$ (or $\frac{3}{8}$) of the cashews are left.

Day 15/Page 31: 1. 1,782; 2. 3,777; 3. 1,786; 4. 5,408; 5. 1,089; 6. 4,593; 7. 33,802; 8. 53,668; 9. no; 10. yes; 11. yes; 12. no; 13. yes; 14. yes; 15. $3\frac{3}{4}$; 16. $1\frac{1}{8}$; 17. $4\frac{4}{5}$; 18. 4; 19. $3\frac{1}{9}$; 20. $1\frac{1}{2}$; 21. $1\frac{1}{7}$; 22. $1\frac{1}{7}$; 23. $3\frac{2}{11}$; Answers will vary, but students' responses should include dialogue.

Day 16/Page 33: 1. went; 2. are; 3. hid; 4. rode; 5. digging; 6. $\frac{25}{100}$; 7. $\frac{55}{100}$; 8. $\frac{92}{100}$; 9. $\frac{50}{100}$; 10. $\frac{93}{100}$; 11. $\frac{95}{100}$

; 12. $\frac{37}{100}$; 13. $\frac{85}{100}$; 14. $\frac{74}{100}$; 15. $\frac{44}{100}$; 16. $\frac{72}{100}$; 17. $\frac{36}{100}$; 18. 3,786; 19. 10,725; 20. 2,976; 21. 29,291; 22. 92,685; 23. 15,255; 24. 22,316; 25. 15,011; 26. >; 27. <; 28. <; 29. >; 30. =; 31. >; 32. >; 33. <; 34. <; 35. =; 36. >; 37. <

Day 17/Page 35: 1.–6. Answers will vary.; 7. aboard, about, above, affect, afford; 8. after, aggravate, agree, aid, ailment; 9. how spiders were created; 10. Arachne and Athena are both talented weavers. Arachne is boastful. Athena is powerful, because she is a goddess.; 11. to say something in a mocking or scornful way; 12. Answers will vary.

Day 18/Page 37: 1. 13 cm; 2. 36 yd.; 3. 10 cups; 4. 12 km; 5. 25 kg; 6. 2 tons; 7. 14 L; 8. 5 mi.; 9. 14 gal.; 10. 10 m; 11. 25 lbs.; 12. 800 cm; 13.–20. Answers will vary.; Stories will vary.

Day 19/Page 39: 1. to stay healthy; 2. whether you are a girl or boy, how active you are, and your age; 3.–4. Answers will vary.; 5. Emmett, Hugo, Boy Scouts; 6. Idaho, Rashad, Snake River; 7. Sierra, Winn Elementary School; 8. Doug, Brookstown Mall; 9. Ms. Hernandez's, Lincoln Memorial, Washington, D.C.; 10. Niagara Falls, Canada; 11. $2.27; 12. $20.40; 13. $45; 14. $7.00; 15. now in progress; 16. information, awareness, understanding; 17. doubt; 18. leaving no room for error, accurate; 19. a kind of lamp; 20. occupation, source of livelihood; 21. worldwide, understood by all; 22. the science and art of farming; 23. to make clearly known

Day 20/Page 41: 1. $3\frac{2}{3}$; 2. $1\frac{1}{8}$; 3. $2\frac{2}{3}$; 4. $2\frac{1}{2}$; 5. $1\frac{3}{4}$; 6. $3\frac{1}{3}$; 7. $1\frac{1}{10}$; 8. $1\frac{3}{7}$; 9. $2\frac{3}{8}$; 10. $2\frac{1}{2}$; 11.

$1\frac{4}{5}$; 12. $3\frac{1}{10}$; 13. $2\frac{3}{10}$; 14. $2\frac{1}{8}$; 15. $4\frac{1}{3}$; Drawings will vary.; 16.–21. Answers will vary.

Bonus Page 46: 1. 55, 11; 2. 50, 10; 3. 20, 4; 4. 40, 8; 5. 30, 6; 6. 20, 4; 7. 90, 18; 8. 50, 10

Bonus Page 47: 1. 1:00 P.M.; 2. 1:00 P.M.; 3. 10:00 A.M.; 4. 4:00 P.M.; 5. 10:00 A.M.

Section II

Day 1/Page 51: Answers will vary.

Day 2/Page 53: 1. 72; 2. 48; 3. 132; 4. 36; 5. 92; 6. 161; 7. 204; 8. 80; 9. 390; 10. 602; 11. F; 12. C; 13. R; 14. C; 15. R; 16. F; Answers will vary. Possible answers: Alice went to the YMCA on Friday afternoon.; Bryson went to the waterpark on Saturday. He went to the library on Sunday.; 17. 2, 3, 4, 5, 6; 18. 3, 40, 4, 50, 5, 60, 6; 19. 2, 18, 4, 30, 6; 20. 6 R9; 21. 6 R36; 22. 6 R24; 23. 9 R11; 24. 4 R6; 25. 5 R8; 26. 9 R33; 27. 4 R12

Day 3/Page 55: 1. 0.25; 2. 0.20; 3. 0.86; 4. 0.37; 5. 0.09; 6. 1.93; 7. 7.15; 8. 15.47; 9. 46.89; 10. 35.06; 11. 625.12; Answers will vary. Possible answers: 12. gorgeous, lovely; 13. hate, abhor; 14. brave, fearless; 15. watch, stare; 16. odd, strange; 17. interesting, enthralling; 18. >; 19. >; 20. >; 21. =; 22. >; 23. <; 24. >; 25. >; 26. <; 27. =; 28. =; 29. <; 30. F, I; 31. I, F; 32. F, I

Day 4/Page 57: 1.–4. Answers will vary.; Students' writing will vary.; 5. a; 6. They make sure that everyone follows the laws of the community to keep people safe.; 7. They put out fires and educate people about fire safety.; 8. The author gives several examples of how different types of people help a community run smoothly.

Day 5/Page 59: 1. 40; 2. 3,600; 3. 5,600; 4. 240; 5. 100; 6. 4,000; 7. 720; 8. 300; 9. 3,000 10. 400; 11. 560; 12. 3,500; 13. 6,300; 14. 2,400; 15. 3,600; 16. 7,200; 17. 1,600; 18. 6,300; 19. 30; 20. 4,200; 21. 2,400; 22. 280; 23. 90; 24. 1,000; 25. right; 26. crying; 27. boils; 28. saved; 29. bird; 30. grow; 31. eggs; 32. well; 33. birch; 34. three; 35. holly; 36. birch; 37. brown, creamy white, dark gray, ash; 38. maple; 39. Answers will vary.

Day 6/Page 61:

×	1	10	100	1,000
1	1	10	100	1,000
2	2	20	200	2,000
3	3	30	300	3,000
4	4	40	400	4,000
5	5	50	500	5,000
6	6	60	600	6,000
7	7	70	700	7,000
8	8	80	800	8,000
9	9	90	900	9,000

Multiplying by hundreds adds one more zero.; 1. you're; 2. your; 3. it's; 4. Its; 5. your; 6. Its; 7. b; 8. People gather for a special meal and a reading of Burns's poetry.; 9. Students' research and writing will vary.

Day 7/Page 63: 1. 700 (2 zeros); 2. 390 (1 zero); 3. 9,000 (3 zeros); 4. 36,000 (3 zeros); 5. 6,000 (3 zeros); 6. 4,600 (2 zeros); 7. 56,000 (3 zeros); 8. 250,000 (4 zeros); 9. 54,000 (3 zeros); 10. 132,000 (3 zeros); 11. 420,000 (4 zeros); 12. 5; 13. 2; 14. 1; 15. 4; 16. 3; 17. She is not telling the truth.; 18. Do you think we'll be in trouble?; 19. You do not notice time passing when you are busy doing something you enjoy.; 20. Shanice got right to the point.; 21. He will help out.; 22. 2,691; 23. 1,296; 24. 3,060; 25. 2,001; 26. 3,542; 27. 2,793; 28. 2,993; 29. 4,560; 30. 5,808; 31. 6,256

Day 8/Page 65: soil; 1. 2,994; 2. 4,249; 3. 4,677; 4. 11,035; 5. 12,979; 6. 3,304; 7. 10,165; 8. 5,785; 9. 2,085; 10. 11,155; 11. 10,020; 12. 2,073; 13. 3, 30, 300; 14. 4, 40, 400; 15. 3, 30, 300; 16. 2, 20, 200; 17. 5, 50, 500; 18. 9, 90, 900; 19. 4, 40, 400; 20. 7, 70, 700; Answers will vary. Possible answers: 21. natural; 22. bold; 23. clockwise; 24. clumsy; 25. common; 26. discourage; 27. wide

Day 9/Page 67: 1. 31 R2; 2. 11 R3; 3. 21 R1; 4. 11 R3; 5. 32 R1; 6. 11 R1; 7. 11 R2; 8. 11 R2; 9. har/ness; 10. live/li/ness; 11. in/flate; 12. ca/ble; 13. glo/ri/ous; 14. wash/ing; 15. pi/geon; 16. ap/ple; 17. jew/el/ry; 18. ma/ple; 19. bi/cy/cle; 20. fro/zen; 21. dif/fi/cult; 22. ten/nis; 23. hap/py; Students' writing will vary.

Day 10/Page 69: 1. $\frac{5}{8}$; 2. $\frac{1}{3}$; 3. $\frac{1}{2}$; 4. $5\frac{1}{5}$; 5. $6\frac{2}{3}$; 6. $4\frac{1}{9}$; 7.–10. Answers will vary.; Answers will vary. Possible answers: 11. "How it clatters along the roofs, Like the tramp of hoofs" He compares the sound of the rain and the sound of hoof beats.; 12. It has been a long time since it has rained. He thinks it is beautiful.; 13. He is grateful for the rain, so his tone is joyful. Oh, the rain, the dreadful rain. Gloomy and gray through the window pane.

Day 11/Page 71: 1. 34.5; 2. 2,732; 3. 625; 4. 25,435; 5. 0.17; 6. 980; 7. 459,760; 8. 1,852.6; 9. 1,005.3; 10. 78,287; 11.–13. Answers will vary.; 14. right; 15. obtuse; 16. acute; 17. obtuse; 18. acute; 19. right

Day 12/Page 73: 1. 3,048; 2. 1,092; 3. 6,336; 4. 5,310; 5. 6,528; 6. 7,000; 7. 6,290; 8. 12,865; 9. 14,616; 10. Lin, Paco, Julie, and Keesha are going to a movie.; 11. Anna took her spelling, reading, and math books to school.; 12. The snack bar is only open Monday, Tuesday, Friday, and Saturday.; 13. Our new school flag is blue, green, yellow, black, and orange.; 14. Many women,

men, children, and pets enjoy sledding.; 15. Have you seen the kittens, chicks, or goslings?; 16. a; 17. put seed in a bird feeder or hang a birdhouse; 18. Answers will vary but may include: What birds like to eat or how they develop over time.; 19. binoculars

Day 13/Page 75: 1. has taken; 2. had noticed; 3. has been; 4. had read; 5. will have earned; 6. had delivered; 7. will have thanked; 8. have been calling; 9. 214 R10; 10. 201 R25; 11. 277 R4; 12. 70 R8; 13. 131; 14. 132; 15. 203 R6; 16. 130 R15; 17. 253 R8; 18. into the pitcher, where; 19. beneath the glossy green leaf, where; 20. across the street, where; 21. during the performance, when; 22. After the game, when; 23. in the stream, where; 24. outside the lines, where; 25. between you and me, where

Day 14/Page 77: 1.–5. Answers will vary.; 6. Yes, I will go with you, Tristan.; 7. Wynona, I am glad Zoe will come.; 8. Aaron, do you play tennis?; 9. Yes, I went to the doctor's office.; 10. Raul, do you want to go?; 11. Neyla, what happened?; 12. No, I never learned how to fish.; 13. Mom, thanks for the help.; 14. No, I need to finish this.; 15. Hugo, I found a penny.; 16. Come on, T.J., let's go to the game.; 17. Tell me, Crystal, did you do this?; Students' writing will vary.

Day 15/Page 79: 1. 36; 2. 5; 3. 24; 4. 5; 5. 21; 6. 8; 7. 4; 8. 700; 9. 171; 10. 7; 11. 36; 12. 40; 13. "Nate, do you have the map of our town?" asked Kit.; 14. "What an exciting day I had!" cried Janelle.; 15. I said, "The puppy chewed up my sneaker."; 16. "Did you know that birds' bones are hollow?" asked Mrs. Tyler.; 17. She answered, "No, I did not know that."; 18. Wayne exclaimed, "I won first prize in the pie-baking contest!"; 19. "I'm tired after raking the yard," said Sadie.; 20. "I am too," replied Sarah.; 21. a; 22. the instruments they use and the results they find; 23. Everyone learns more about the subjects.; 24. to make sure that you are being safe

Day 16/Page 81: 1. St. Patrick's Day; 2. Valentine's Day; 3. Independence Day; 4. Halloween; 5. Labor Day; 6. January; 7. Father's Day; 8. braid; 9. list; 10. moon; 11. world; 12. gondola; 13. spray; 14. flash; 15. certain; 16. genuine, great; 17. terrible, straight; 18. among, awhile; 19. where, weather; 20. junior, journey; 21. remain, refer; 22. feathers, fiction; 23. drawer, detective; 24. holiday, healthy; 25. explore, enormous; 26. but; 27. Both/and; 28. After; 29. Neither/nor; 30. and; 31.Since

Day 17/Page 83: 1. 2; 2. 8; 3. 6; 4. 2; 5. 2; 6. 10; 7. 6; 8. 3; 9. 8; 10. 0; 11. 3; 12. 5; 13. 2; 14. 1; 15. 10; 16. 8; 17. artificial; 18. schedule; 19. exchange; 20. reputation; 21. assistant; 22. genuine; 23. campaign; 24. publicize; 25. A man writes to his brother to try to convince him to come west during the Gold Rush.; 26. Answers will vary. Possible answer: The reader might not have such a clear picture of what it was really like to go West in the hopes of striking it rich. 27. He is pleased with his decision and wants his brother to join him.

Day 18/Page 85: 1. Charlie and the Chocolate Factory; 2. The Lego Movie; 3. Where the Sidewalk Ends; 4. "This Land Is Your Land"; 5. Romeo and Juliet; 6. "Afternoon on a Hill"; 7. "Let It Go", Frozen; 8. Miracle on 34th Street; 9. 6; 10. 2; 11. 2; 12. 3; 13. 5; 14. 7; 15.–17. Answers will vary.; Students' writing will vary.

Day 19/Page 87: 1.–6. Answers will vary. 7. 1.36; 8. 4.023; 9. 0.5; 10. 0.47; 11. 0.833; 12. 0.12; 0.12, 0.47, 0.5, 0.833, 1.36, 4.023; Students' writing will vary.; 13. $\frac{3}{8}$; 14. 2; 15. $\frac{15}{56}$; 16. $2\frac{3}{4}$; 17. $\frac{2}{9}$; 18. $\frac{12}{25}$; 19. $\frac{5}{9}$; 20. $2\frac{1}{4}$; 21. $\frac{8}{49}$; 22. $4\frac{4}{5}$; 23. $\frac{1}{9}$; 24. 7

Day 20/Page 89: 1. recites, recited; 2. loved, love; 3. met, will meet; 4. will dry, dried; 5. is, will be; 6. was, is; 7. $\frac{1}{4}$ of the field; 8. $\frac{1}{5}$ of the cars; 9. $\frac{1}{3}$ of the pizza; 10. $\frac{1}{5}$ of the marbles; 11. a; 12. c; 13. b; 14. a; 15. d; Students' writing will vary.

Bonus Page 93: 1. a; 2. a; 3. b; 4. a

Bonus Page 94: 1. b; 2. Alice Springs; 3. Melbourne; 4. Great Barrier Reef; 5. Perth

Bonus Page 95: 1. d; 2. c; 3. a; 4. b

Section III

Day 1/Page 99: 1. Both/and; 2. Either/or; 3. both/and; 4. Not only/but also; 5. Neither/nor; 6. Both/and; 7. a; 8. Greenwich, England; 9. people who study geography and mapmaking and explorers around the world; 10. Answers will vary.

Day 2/Page 101:

1. 10; 2. $\frac{1}{40}$; 3. $\frac{1}{28}$; 4. 9; 5. 18; 6. $\frac{1}{24}$

; 7. 45; 8. $\frac{1}{30}$; 9. $\frac{1}{12}$; 10. 16; 11. 14; 12. $\frac{1}{27}$

July 17, 2015

Dear David,

Thank you for sending me the pictures from your trip. It looks like you had a great time! Do you want me to send them back?

Next week, I'm going to Kansas City with my dad. I can't wait!

Your friend,

Greg

Day 3/Page 103: 1. (15 − 7) ÷ 2 = 4; 2. (56 ÷ 8) × 4 = 28; 3. (5 × 9) − 12 = 33; 4. (12 ÷ 2) × (3 + 2) = 30; 5. (8 − 1) × (3 × 3) = 63; 6. (24 ÷ 8) + 10 = 13; Students' writing will vary.; 7. b; 8. groups of people who feel the same way about one or more issues; 9. Answers will vary.; 10. rose, oak tree, dove

Day 4/Page 105: 1. 10; 2. 80; 3. 10,000; 4. 144; 5. 2; 6. 14,000; 7. 4; 8. 176; 9. 6,000; 10. 20,000; 11. 2; 12. 48; 13. $1\frac{3}{8}$; 14. $1\frac{1}{18}$; 15. $\frac{8}{15}$; 16. $2\frac{1}{3}$; 17. $2\frac{1}{12}$; 18. $\frac{28}{39}$; 19. $\frac{23}{60}$; 20. $1\frac{5}{8}$; 21. $\frac{33}{70}$; 22. cells; 23. water; 24. iron, calcium; 25. digestive; 26. circulatory; 27.–32. Answers will vary, but may include: 27. bumpy, smooth; 28. trouble, solution; 29. fascinating, boring; 30. shock, expectation; 31. cheerful, sad; 32. collect, plant

Day 5/Page 107: 1. quietquippers. joke; 2. ruhilarious.joke; 3. 36,959 visitors; 4. 12,455 visitors; 5. 9,129 visitors; 6. 61,593 visitors; 7. c; 8. the outlines of the continents and seas; 9. important buildings and streets; 10. north, south, east, and west

Day 6/Page 109: 1. 6,843,000; 2. 906,400,002; 3. nine hundred eighty-six million two hundred eighteen thousand three hundred twenty; 4. two hundred thirty-four million one hundred eighty-six thousand eighteen; Poems will vary.; 5. Answers will vary. Possible answer: He wore tents as diapers. It took a herd of cows to fill his belly with milk. He flooded towns by playing in the ocean.; 6. to entertain; the tone is funny and amusing; 7. Answers will vary.

Day 7/Page 111: 1. $2\frac{1}{8}$ hours; 2. 1 $\frac{8}{15}$ pounds; 3. $4\frac{1}{6}$ cups; 4. 1 $\frac{23}{24}$ miles; 5. teknique, technique; 6. migrasion, migration; 7. Febuary, February; 8. impashent, impatient; 9. scisors, scissors; 10. seperate, separate; 11. girl; 12. king; 13. eat; 14. tree; 15. pilot; 16. jar; 17. break; Students' writing will vary.

Day 8/Page 113: 1. Unfortunately, the package did not arrive in time.; 2. Although Hannah was near the front of the line, she did not get to choose the book she wanted.; 3. On Saturday, Dad is going to make pancakes for breakfast.; 4. At the corner of Wilcox Road and Pinevale Avenue, there is a fruit stand.; 5. Sadly, we were not able to rescue the baby bird.; 6. In spite of the rain, the festival was a lot of fun.; 7. To get to the pond, take Dragonfly Trail.; 8. First, stretch your arms above your head as far as you can reach.; 9. Students should cross out the circle.; 10. Students should cross out the square or rectangle.; 11. Students should cross out the square or rectangle.; 12. Students should cross out the right triangle.; 13. Students should cross out the hexagon.; 14. Students should cross out the triangle.; 15. Students should circle the trapezoid.; 16. because Tiger always keeps his paws clean; 17. The story is told from third-person point of view. It works well for this story because it tells what different people and animals are doing instead of focusing on one character.; 18. Paragraphs will vary.

Day 9/Page 115: 1. Olivia; 2. Isabella; 3. $25; 4. $30; 5. Lonny and Ava; 6. $72.50; 7. unhappy; 8. preheat; 9. bicycle; 10. review; 11. misunderstand; 12. unknown; 13. uncover; 14. uniform; 15. replace; 16. $159.92; 17. $44.22; 18. $142.50; 19. $3.23; 20. $348.81; 21. $7.11; 22. $1,005.12; 23. $57.42; 24. to look forward to; 25. a situation; 26. obvious; 27. easily noticed; 28. a place of shelter and protection; 29. to keep in check; repress

Day 10/Page 117: 1. Nutrients; 2. Exercise; 3. water; 4. food groups; 5. energy; 6. healthy; 7.–16. Answers will vary.;

There would be $22\frac{1}{8}$ quarts of soil in each pot.; 17. Mrs. Zheng planted zinnias, cosmos, poppies, and bluebells in her wildflower garden.; 18. This week, we have seen cardinals, chickadees, sparrows, and robins at the feeder.; 19. Darius invited Erik, Joey, Roberto, and Sam to sleep over on Saturday.; 20. Please remember to get broccoli, cheddar cheese, orange juice, and bread at the grocery store.; 21. Malia brought watercolors, paintbrushes, and a pad of paper to her art class.; 22. Sadie won a goldfish, a teddy bear, and a plastic bracelet at the carnival.

Day 11/Page 119: 1. 90 cubic feet; 2. 36 cubic yards; 3. 60 cubic yards; 4. 15 cubic feet; Answers will vary, but may include: My friend and I visited Cardiff, Wales. **We** learned that Cardiff is the capital and largest port of Wales. **T**he city lies on the River Taff near the Bristol Channel. Cardiff is near the largest coal mines in Great Britian.; 5. b; 6. slim, needle-like parts; 7. sunlight, air, water, and minerals; 8. They help attract bees and butterflies, which bring pollen.

Day 12/Page 121: Students' writing will vary.; 1. $\frac{3}{10}$ or 0.3; 2. $\frac{9}{10}$ or 0.9; 3. $\frac{8}{10}$ or 0.8; 4. $\frac{2}{10}$ or 0.2; 5. $\frac{4}{10}$ or 0.4; 6. 0.2; 7. 1.1; 8. 6.4; 9. $8\frac{5}{10}$; 10. $\frac{9}{10}$; 11. $10\frac{6}{10}$; Pictures will vary.

Day 13/Page 123: 1. B; 2. A; 3. B; 4. A; 5. B; 6. 50; 7. 8,000; 8. 6,000; 9. 12; 10. 8,000; 11. 12,000; 12. 5,000; 13. 17; 14. 4; 15. 12,000; 16. 100; 17. 1; 18. a; 19. San Diego has a very mild climate, and New Orleans is humid.; 20. Climate describes the weather in an area over a long period of time.; 21. Climates near the equator are warmer than those at the poles.

Day 14/Page 125: 1. runs; 2. catches; 3. goes; 4. dove; 5. visited; 6. went; 7. will read; 8. will show; 9. will wash; Students' writing will vary.; 10. a; 11. They are fuels made from things like vegetable oil and are used like fossil fuels.; 12. Biodiesel burns more cleanly than diesel fuel. Biofuel is a renewable resource.

Day 15/Page 127:

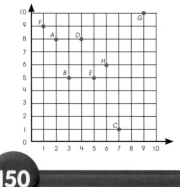

1. M; 2. S; 3. M; 4. S; 5. P; 6. M; 7. P; 8. a; 9. obey the laws of their country, respect the opinions of others, help others in their community; 10. 18 years old; 11. right to a fair trial, right to speak freely, and right to practice any religion

Day 16/Page 129: 1. $15.60; 2. $18.72; 3. $12.22; 4. $11.25; 5. $27.54; 6. $31.86; 7. $119.68; 8. $193.20; 9. Walter; 10. Gerald; 11. Alejandro; 12. Ian; 13. Dad; 14. Betsy; 15. Donna; 16. Tara; 17. 60 m³; 18. 160 in.³; 19. 41.354 m³; 20. 240 mm³; 21. 38.4 in.³; 22. 384 cm³

Day 17/Page 131: 1. 6 pounds; 2. $1\frac{1}{2}$ cups; 3. $4\frac{2}{5}$ feet; 4. $\frac{21}{32}$ mile; Students' paragraphs will vary.; 5. 2 cups; 6. 60 gal.; 7. 2 gal.; 8. 10; 9. 2; 10. 4; 11. 2; 12. 12; 13. 4

Day 18/Page 133: 1. 55,364.9; 2. 476.82; 3. 208,036,408; 4. 2,101.536; 5. 400,250.086; 6. 307,000,205.111; 7. $(1 \times 100,000) + (2 \times 10,000) + (6 \times 1,000) + (5 \times 100) + (5 \times 10) + (2 \times 1) + (2 \times \frac{1}{10}) + (5 \times \frac{1}{100}) + (4 \times \frac{1}{1,000})$; 8. $(7 \times 1,000,000) + (5 \times 100,000) + (2 \times 10,000) + (6 \times 100) + (3 \times 10) + (4 \times 1) + (4 \times \frac{1}{10}) + (8 \times \frac{1}{100})$; 9. The book was ripped **because** the dog chewed it.; 10. **Because** it was so cold, Betty could ice-skate for only a short while.; 11. I went to bed early last night **because** I was so tired.; 12. **Because** it was raining hard, we couldn't play outside.; 13. The rabbit ran away quickly **because** it saw a cat.; 14. It was very foggy outside, **so** we could not see the mountains.; 15. **Because** we got to camp too late, there was no time for hiking.; 16. c; 17. items that are produced; 18. books and clothing; 19. activities that people do for one another; 20. teacher

and police officer

Day 19/Page 135:

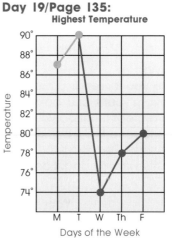

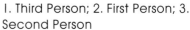

1. Third Person; 2. First Person; 3. Second Person

Day 20/Page 137:

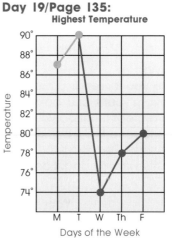

1. a; 2. the citizens of that city; 3. make the laws that everyone must follow; 4. police officers, firefighters, mayor

Bonus Page 140: 1. solar; 2. new moon; 3. umbra

Bonus Page 141: 1. d; 2. c; 3. c; 4. a

Bonus Page 142: 1. d; 2. b; 3. b

Bonus Page 143: 1. b; 2. d; 3. c; 4. d; 5. b

piece

© Carson-Dellosa

accept

© Carson-Dellosa

threw

© Carson-Dellosa

weather

© Carson-Dellosa

their

© Carson-Dellosa

presents

© Carson-Dellosa

patience

© Carson-Dellosa

principle

© Carson-Dellosa

peace

© Carson-Dellosa

calm	peaceful	tranquil
© Carson-Dellosa	© Carson-Dellosa	© Carson-Dellosa
destroy	wreck	ruin
© Carson-Dellosa	© Carson-Dellosa	© Carson-Dellosa
fantastic	amazing	incredible
© Carson-Dellosa	© Carson-Dellosa	© Carson-Dellosa

except

through

whether

they're

presence

patients

principal

response

reply

powerful	answer	weak
© Carson-Dellosa	© Carson-Dellosa	© Carson-Dellosa
wild	tame	defeat
© Carson-Dellosa	© Carson-Dellosa	© Carson-Dellosa
triumph	admire	despise
© Carson-Dellosa	© Carson-Dellosa	© Carson-Dellosa

graph
(draw or write)

scope
(look at or examine)

vis
(see)

tri
(three)

audi
(hearing, sound)

cent
(hundred)

ject
(throw)

meter
(measure)

port
(carry)

invisible
visual
supervisor

© Carson-Dellosa

telescope
stethoscope
microscope

© Carson-Dellosa

geography
photograph
phonograph

© Carson-Dellosa

century
percent
centennial

© Carson-Dellosa

audience
auditorium
audition

© Carson-Dellosa

triathlete
tricycle
trillion

© Carson-Dellosa

transport
export
portable

© Carson-Dellosa

thermometer
perimeter
speedometer

© Carson-Dellosa

projection
inject
objection

© Carson-Dellosa

$\frac{1}{2}$ of 8 multiplied
by the sum of 5
and 6

© Carson-Dellosa

auto
(self)

© Carson-Dellosa

rupt
(break)

© Carson-Dellosa

the quotient of
24 and 8
multiplied by 5

© Carson-Dellosa

12 more than
the quotient
of 36 and 6

© Carson-Dellosa

the difference
of 20 and 5
divided by 3

© Carson-Dellosa

$10 \times [6 + (30 \div 3)]$

© Carson-Dellosa

9 less than the
product of
3 and 10

© Carson-Dellosa

the difference of
16 and 5 multiplied
by the product of
4 and 2

© Carson-Dellosa

erupt
interruption
disrupt

© Carson-Dellosa

---

automobile
autobiography
automatic

© Carson-Dellosa

$(\frac{1}{2} \times 8) \times (5 + 6)$

© Carson-Dellosa

$(20 - 5) \div 3$

© Carson-Dellosa

$(36 \div 6) + 12$

© Carson-Dellosa

$(24 \div 8) \times 5$

© Carson-Dellosa

$(16 - 5) \times (4 \times 2)$

© Carson-Dellosa

$(3 \times 10) - 9$

© Carson-Dellosa

$10 \times [6 + (30 \div 3)]$
$= 160$

© Carson-Dellosa

3.5 x 10 =

© Carson-Dellosa

[6 + (23 × 3)] ÷ 3

© Carson-Dellosa

2 × {3 × [9 + (7 − 2)]}

© Carson-Dellosa

35 ÷ 10 =

© Carson-Dellosa

3.5 x 1,000 =

© Carson-Dellosa

3.5 x 100 =

© Carson-Dellosa

364.87

© Carson-Dellosa

35 ÷ 1,000 =

© Carson-Dellosa

35 ÷ 100 =

© Carson-Dellosa

$3.5 \times 10 = 35$

$[6 + (23 \times 3)] \div 3$
$= 25$

$2 \times \{3 \times [9 + (7 - 2)]\}$
$= 84$

$35 \div 10 = 3.5$

$3.5 \times 1,000 =$
$3,500$

$3.5 \times 100 = 350$

$(3 \times 100) + (6 \times 10)$
$+ (4 \times 1) + (8 \times \frac{1}{10})$
$+ (7 \times \frac{1}{100})$

$35 \div 1,000 =$
$.035$

$35 \div 100 =$
0.35

72.589

© Carson-Dellosa

521.134

© Carson-Dellosa

$$\frac{1}{3} = \frac{\square}{9}$$

© Carson-Dellosa

$$\frac{1}{4} = \frac{\square}{16}$$

© Carson-Dellosa

$$\frac{2}{3} = \frac{\square}{12}$$

© Carson-Dellosa

$$\frac{6}{8} = \frac{\square}{24}$$

© Carson-Dellosa

$$\frac{3}{4} = \frac{\square}{12}$$

© Carson-Dellosa

$$\frac{1}{2} = \frac{\square}{8}$$

© Carson-Dellosa

$$4 \times \frac{3}{4} =$$

© Carson-Dellosa

$\frac{1}{3} = \frac{3}{9}$

© Carson-Dellosa

$(5 \times 100) + (2 \times 10) +$
$(1 \times 1) + (1 \times \frac{1}{10}) +$
$(3 \times \frac{1}{100}) + (4 \times \frac{1}{1000})$

© Carson-Dellosa

$(7 \times 10) + (2 \times 1) +$
$(5 \times \frac{1}{10}) + (8 \times \frac{1}{100})$
$+ (9 \times \frac{1}{1000})$

© Carson-Dellosa

$\frac{6}{8} = \frac{18}{24}$

© Carson-Dellosa

$\frac{2}{3} = \frac{8}{12}$

© Carson-Dellosa

$\frac{1}{4} = \frac{4}{16}$

© Carson-Dellosa

$4 \times \frac{3}{4} = \frac{12}{4}$ or 3

© Carson-Dellosa

$\frac{1}{2} = \frac{4}{8}$

© Carson-Dellosa

$\frac{3}{4} = \frac{9}{12}$

© Carson-Dellosa

$$\frac{2}{3} \times \frac{4}{7} =$$

© Carson-Dellosa

$$\frac{1}{4} \times \frac{1}{3} =$$

© Carson-Dellosa

$$\frac{3}{4} \times \frac{1}{6} =$$

© Carson-Dellosa

$$\frac{5}{8} \times \frac{2}{3} =$$

© Carson-Dellosa

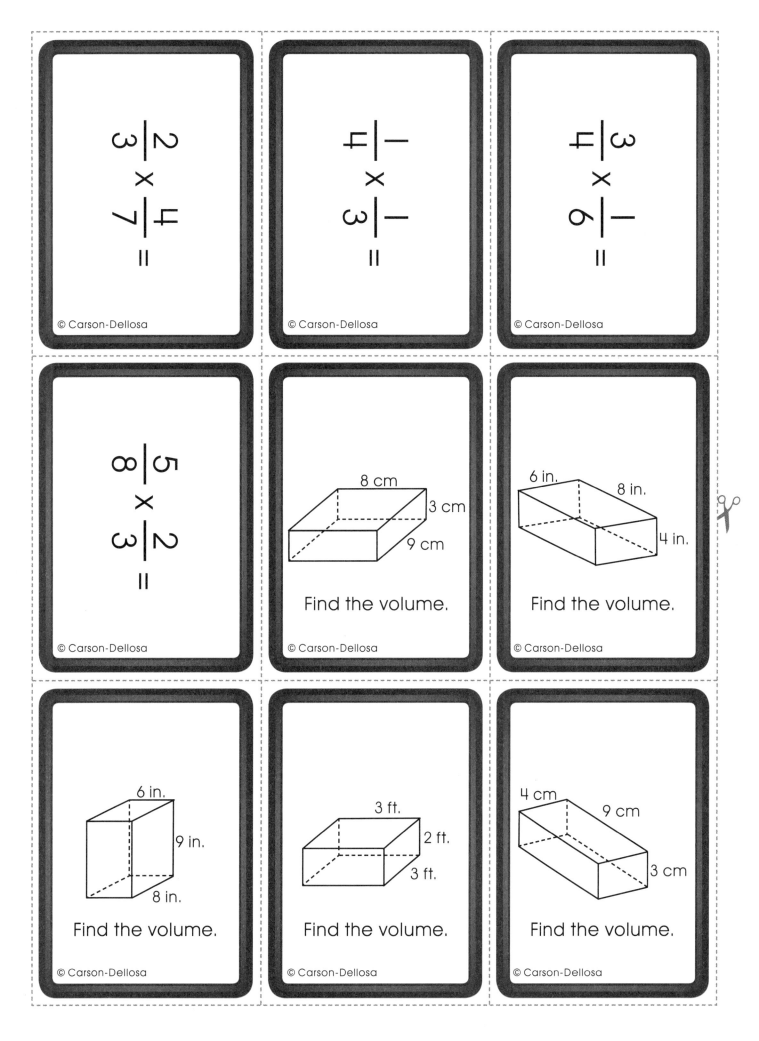

Find the volume.

© Carson-Dellosa

Find the volume.

© Carson-Dellosa

Find the volume.

© Carson-Dellosa

Find the volume.

© Carson-Dellosa

Find the volume.

© Carson-Dellosa

$\dfrac{2}{3} \times \dfrac{4}{7} = \dfrac{8}{21}$

$\dfrac{1}{4} \times \dfrac{1}{3} = \dfrac{1}{12}$

$\dfrac{3}{4} \times \dfrac{1}{6} = \dfrac{3}{24}$ or $\dfrac{1}{8}$

$\dfrac{5}{8} \times \dfrac{2}{3} = \dfrac{10}{24}$ or $\dfrac{5}{12}$

Volume = 216 cubic cm

Volume = 192 cubic in.

Volume = 432 cubic in.

Volume = 18 cubic ft.

Volume = 108 cubic cm

Summer Bridge Activities®

Congratulations!

This certifies that

_____

Name

has completed **Summer Bridge Activities**.

_____

Parent's Signature